100 GREATS DURHAM COUNTY CRICKET CLUB

100 GREATS

DURHAM
COUNTY CRICKET CLUB

COMPILED BY
MATTHEW APPLEBY

TEMPUS

Acknowledgements

Don Ambrose, Edgar Appleby, James Bailey, Ray Baker, Harry Bell, James Bielby, Robert Brooke, Simon Brown, Lance Cairns, Paul Collingwood, Geoff Cook, Alec Coxon, George Crawford, Clive Crickmer, David Graveney, Walter Hadlee, Stephen Harmison, James Howarth, Brian Hunt, Andy Jarvis, Brian Lander, Dennis Lambert, Eddie Lawrence, Leicestershire CCC, Jonathan Lewis, Paul McGregor, John Morris, David O'Sullivan, Ashok Patel, William Powell, Craig Ray, Malcolm Scott, Martin Speight, Michael Tate, Vince Wells, Stuart Wilkinson, Gus Williamson, John Wood, *Northern Echo*, Lennard Associates, Tempus Publishing.

Key

Bowling

O	overs
Md	maidens
R	runs conceded
W	wickets
Ave	bowling average
5wI	five wickets in an innings
10wM	ten wickets in a match
ct	caught
st	stumped

Batting

M	Matches played
I	innings
NO	not outs
Runs	runs
Ave	batting average
100s	centuries
50s	fifties

Positions

RHB	right hand bat
LHB	left hand bat
RF	right arm fast bowler
RFM	right fast medium bowler
RM	right arm medium bowler
SLA	slow left arm bowler
OB	off break bowler
LB	leg break bowler

Other abbreviations

BHC	Benson and Hedges Cup
CC	Cricket Club
CCC	County Cricket Club
DSCL	Durham Senior Cricket League
DSO	Distinguished Service Order
ESCA	English Schools Cricket Association

GC	Gillette Cup
HM	Her Majesty's Forces
MA	Master of Arts
MCC	Marylebone Cricket Club
MCCA	Minor Counties Cricket Association
NUL	Norwich Union League
NWT	Natwest Trophy
NYSD	North Yorkshire and South Durham League
ODI	One Day International
SL	Sunday League
TCCB	Test and County Cricket Board

Post-1992 players first-class record for Durham only
Pre-1992 includes all Durham games
Figures to end 2003 season

First published 2004

Tempus Publishing Limited
The Mill, Brimscombe Port,
Stroud, Gloucestershire, GL5 2QG
www.tempus-publishing.com

© Matthew Appleby, 2004

The right of Matthew Appleby to be identified as the Author
of this work has been asserted in accordance with the
Copyrights, Designs and Patents Act 1988.

British Library Cataloguing in Publication Data.
A catalogue record for this book is available from the British Library.

ISBN 0 7524 3195 1

Typesetting and origination by Tempus Publishing Limited
Printed and bound in Great Britain

Foreword

James Lowe 2003 -? The entry will not mean too much to the circles outside of the Lowe family and Durham members but that is the very latest addition to Durham's first-class records. They number seventy-seven in all, and are following in the footsteps of those who represented the minor county between 1882 and 1991.

The history of Durham as a minor county played a major part on achieving first-class status. The current players have a wonderful opportunity to set the standards that future generations will aim to follow. Hopefully, they respect the past and rise to the challenge of the future.

I've had the great honour of welcoming to Durham most of its seventy-seven players, twenty-two of which are included in this book, but many of the other names evoke some personal memories. David Townsend through his many guises, Stephen Atkinson; we were trialists together at Northampton in 1968, just before Ollie's accident. Bobby Cole, Stuart Young and Jack Watson the legends of the NYSD league. Captain Lander, only recently stopped 'putting back' into youth coaching. Ron Aspinall and David Halfyard, first-class umpires and so on.

One of the core aims of Durham is to now contribute significantly to English cricket and already we have welcomed Ian Botham, Simon Brown, Paul Collingwood and Stephen Harmison back into the ranks as England players. The presence of all of these names in the top 100 cannot be disputed but many others will be. Such debates are the very essence of the history of the game.

Geoff Cook

Introduction

Readers will argue as to whether this selection is representative of Durham's best players. It is a hopeless task to make a definitive choice, so I have gone for some of the more interesting characters in among stars such as Ian Botham, David Boon, Stephen Harmison and Paul Collingwood. Politician Lord Gainford, plastic surgeon Freddie Herbert, war hero Tommie Bradford and rugby internationals Charles Young Adamson, Alan Old and Edgar Elliot are six of the men who have made great impressions outside cricket.

Players working in jobs as varied as a Portakabin salesman, plantation manager, colliery keeker, ironmaster, television executive (the job of two of our players), and security guard made up pre-professional Durham teams. Cricket administrator Harry Mallett and invigorating innings-starter Ollie Milburn changed the game in their different ways. Brian Lander's 1973 giant-killers effectively ended Yorkshire's reign as the leading County Championship team. After the match, the players quietly drove home to Durham because they were playing club cricket the next day.

As well as rare personalities, this book also includes rare photographs of players who are not even footnotes in the histories of other counties they played for. Albert Howell, the brother of England and Warwickshire's Harry, who endured war wounds in his back is one such example, as he bowled Durham to a Championship in his first season in the north. Denis Hendren, who taught his brother Patsy the game, is another. Yorkshire cricket histories mention Alec Coxon, the Yorkshire martinet, but only the few able to read between the lines would know his true extraordinary story.

From being underdogs, Durham are now underachievers. Losing Martin Saggers to Kent lost the county 500 cheap wickets and a future test player. Recruiting Simon Brown from a failing county career at Northants, then giving him the chance to lead the attack, created an international.

Such is the newness of Durham first-class status, if this book was written in five years, names such as Bridge, Peng, Muchall, Davies, Plunkett, Mustard and Lowe may be certainties for inclusion.

Nevertheless, entertaining times rolled on. Tales of the antics of Coxon and Ron Aspinall in the 1950s, particularly the Keswick pitch and putt incident, are mirrored by the good times had by Botham and Wayne Larkins in the 1990s.

I am sure many readers will know the stories of many of the players in the hundred. Again, I hope some of the stories are new. This is where Durham differs from the other seventeen first-class counties. As the newest county it has looked forward, ever since Geoff Cook and David Graveney planned 1992's first championship squad. Durham staged its first test match in 2003. It will hold many more, as well as one day internationals and World Cup ties. However, there is always time to look back.

100 Club Greats

Charles Lodge Adamson
Charles Young Adamson
William 'Barney' Anderson
Mohinder Armanath
Ronald Aspinall
Stephen Robert Atkinson
Arthur Whitelock Austin
Harry John Bailey
Philip Bainbridge
Henry Davey Bell
Melvyn Morris Betts
Ken Biddulph
Peter Cresswell Birtwisle
David Clarence Boon
Ian Terence Botham
Robert Bousfield
Col Sir Thomas Andrews
    Bradford DSO
Hubert Brooks
Simon John Emmerson Brown
Alan James Burridge
Bernard Lance Cairns
John Carr
Robert Cole
Paul David Collingwood
Geoffrey Cook
John Cook
Thomas Coulson
Alexander Coxon
George Crawford
Hugh Lloyd Dales
Thomas Kell Dobson
Alexander Graham Doggart
Edgar William Elliot
Stanley Ellis

Henry Cecil Ferens CBE
Andrew Robert Fothergill
Harry Gibbon
John David Glendenen
David Anthony Graveney
Stephen Greensword
John Gregory
David John Halfyard
Donald Wrightson Hardy
Stephen James Harmison
Frank Harry
Denis Hendren
Dr Frederick Ironsides Herbert
Albert Louis Howell
Russell Inglis
Thomas Keith Jackson
John Johnston
Dean Mervyn Jones
John George Keeler
Neil Killeen
Thomas Kinch
Peter Kippax
James Thomas 'Kellet' Kirtley
William Kennedy Laidlaw
Brian Richard Lander
Wayne Larkins
Clive William Leach
Jonathan James Benjamin Lewis
John Wilton Lister
Martin Lloyd Love
Richard Henry Mallett
Richard Anthony David Mercer
Colin Milburn
Alfred Morris
John Edward Morris

Maurice Nichol
Alan Gerald Bernard Old
David O'Sullivan
Norman William Owen
Cecil Harry Parkin
Alan Herring Parnaby
Ashok Sitaram Patel
Joseph Albert Pease
Andrew Pratt
Ernest Barton Proud
Roland Barton Proud
Wasim Hasan Raja
Neil Riddell
Paul William Romaines
Michael Anthony Roseberry
Malcolm Ernest Scott
Nicholas Jason Speak
Martin Peter Speight
Richard Thompson Spooner
Michael Tate
James Thackeray
Alan Townsend
David Charles Humphery
    Townsend
George Turnbull
Jack Watson
Lyndon Herbert Weight
William Fry Whitwell
John Stuart Wilkinson
John Gordon Barkass
    Williamson
John Wood
Stuart Harrison Young

Charles Lodge Adamson

RHB, 1926-45

Charles Lodge Adamson			
Born: Durham, 18 May 1906			
Died: Durham, 18 November 1979			
Batting			
M	I	NO	Runs
111	157	24	4,312
Ave	100	50	Ct
32.42	3	20	36
Best Performance			
137* v. Northumberland, 1933			

Son of Charles Young Adamson, Charles Lodge Adamson was a successful batsman for the county for twenty years, and set a record total of over 10,000 runs for the Durham City club. Adamson's debut season coincided with Durham's first championship since 1900. Maurice Nichol, Len Weight, Jack Carr, Albert Howell and Jack Cook were ever-present and Adamson, Bertie Brooks, Cecil Ferens, Tom Dobson junior and Harry Gibbon missed only eight games between them.

Charlie Adamson was an immaculately turned out, diligently defensive, steady opening batsman who played alongside his younger brother John Alfred from 1929 until after the war, for both Durham City and County. John, born in 1909, was an aggressive bat in 49 matches for Durham, scoring 1715 runs. He won blues for rugby union at Oxford University in 1928, 1929 and 1931, playing in an England trial in 1931.

Charlie and John's grandfather, John, was born in Little Grant County, Wisconsin. He was an early part of a great tradition of Durham players (playing 16 games scoring 458 runs and taking 18 wickets), who took up the administrative burden before he had finished playing. Adamson was the second Durham CCC President (succeeding Sir Hedworth Williamson, Bart in 1887), Hon. Secretary after Harry Mallett from 1895-97 and Treasurer from 1885-1907.

Adamson, who was vice-captain to Cecil Ferens at Durham City and Durham County, had his best championship years in 1932, with 425 runs (528 overall) and 1933 with 489 runs (582 in all at 83.14, behind only Elliot's average of 84.15 in 1907). In 1933, Adamson stroked his best effort against a touring team, caught by Oscar Da Costa off Manny Martindale for 93, the highest score of a drawn match against the West Indies, which Durham led by 116 runs after the first innings. That season Adamson ended a seven-year gap with two centuries, 100* against Yorkshire II and his highest score, 137* against Northumberland. In 1934 he top scored in both innings in the draw with the Australians, making 23 and 52. In 1930 his 86* in the 301 run challenge match win over Surrey II helped give Durham a second title in five seasons.

An incident in 1936 perhaps illustrates Adamson's character. In the season Adamson passed his father's Durham run record, Sacriston fast bowler Jim Jones, during a spell of 5/10 in 44 deliveries, kissed Adamson, who had taken a catch in the covers off Jones' bowling. Jones never played for Durham again.

Adamson took an appointment as sports master at Barnard Castle School, making fewer appearances for Durham, but still scoring 308 runs at 34.22 in Durham's 18th place finish in 1939. He became headmaster of Bowes School.

Adamson played twice in 1945 in non-championship games before retirement. At his death he had the fourth highest aggregate for the county, behind Russell Inglis, Edgar Elliot and Carr.

Charles Young Adamson

LHB & LM/SLA, 1894-1914

The son of a county mainstay and the father of two more, Charlie Adamson was a rugby international, war hero in South Africa and Europe and one of Durham's early batting greats.

Born at Neville's Cross, where Lord Ralph Neville defeated the Scots in 1346, and educated at Durham School, Adamson played for Durham City during his whole county career. William Whitwell was captain when nineteen-year-old Adamson made his county debut in 1894. Harry Mallett had taken over when Adamson, an enterprising opener, scored his first two Durham centuries, 110 against Surrey II in a friendly at the Oval and 139 against Northants, both in 1897.

An even better rugby player than cricketer, Adamson stayed in Australia after playing as a half-back on the 1899 British Lions rugby tour. The team was captained and managed by Revd Matthew Mullineux, who had never played an England trial, let alone an international, and became the only

Lion to never play in a home international. Mullineux was one of a weak team (only seven players out of 21 were internationals) and dropped himself after one test (lost 13-3), leaving an opening in the half-backs for Adamson, who then scored two tries, four conversions and a penalty in the 3-1 series victory. Adamson then joined the 4th Queensland Mounted Infantry and, like England rugby international 'Tegger' Elliot, fought in the Boer War.

Adamson played in Australia for the Valley club and once for Queensland, in the 1899 Sheffield Shield competition (Colin Milburn was the next Durham player to have that distinction), scoring five in each innings and taking 0/67 with his left arm medium, which he varied with spin depending on the wicket.

After his Australian and Boer War experiences, Adamson returned to Durham and scored 116 against Northumberland in 1910 at Chester-le-Street and, perhaps an even better innings, 65 (out of Durham's 142) against the Australians in 1912 at Ashbrooke. In 1912, his sole year of captaincy following Tom Coulson's resignation, Adamson's Durham beat Lincolnshire and Cheshire in four successive days on tour, but the campaign proved unsuccessful and Adamson played just four more games for the county.

The corn merchant turned local stockbroker joined the 4th Battalion Tyneside Scottish (23rd Battalion Northumberland Fusiliers) as Lieutenant

Charles Young Adamson
Born: Durham, 18 April 1875
Died: Salonika, Greece, 17 September 1918
Also played for: Queensland

Batting

M	I	NO	Runs
96	157	7	3,525
Ave	100	50	
23.50	3	17	

Bowling

O	Md	R	W
561.5	94	1,807	87
Ave	5wI	10wM	Ct
20.77	5	1	37

Best Performances
139 v. Northamptonshire, 1897
8/25 v. Lincolnshire, 1912

Quarter Master on its formation in 1914. Promoted to captain, he transferred to the 29th Battalion, and then went to Salonika with the 8th Battalion of the Royal Scots Fusiliers in 1918, where he was killed in action in the last months of the war.

Charlie's father, John, was a well-known Durham cricket personality and his sons, Charles Lodge and John Alfred, both played for Durham City and County.

William 'Barney' Anderson — 100 GREATS
LHB & LFM, 1883-96

The epitome of the Victorian professional bowler, erstwhile Coldstream Guard Barney Anderson, who played for the Household Brigade with Westoe-born England captain Drewy Stoddart, averaged more than five wickets a match for Durham.

An odd incident shows some of the pressures on the nineteenth-century professional cricketer. When Anderson took his career best, and caught the other two batsmen to see off Sussex for 29, Durham still lost by 237 runs. Anderson had bowled the future Hollywood actor Aubrey Smith and future England player (as was Smith) Fred Tate. However, Anderson celebrated too well that night, something he denied. He took 1/67 in the second innings, but had to bowl with a bound hand after stopping a return drive from Willie Quaife, who hit 86. The pitch had not improved as much

as it seemed, however, as brothers Arthur and Jesse Hide bowled out Durham for 64 in its second innings.

Anderson took either six or seven wickets on his Durham debut in 1883, but club commitments meant he missed 1885-87. By the 1890s Hon. Secretary Harry Mallett was paying Anderson and another professional bowler, Thomas Thompson, £2 a match. Durham engaged Anderson on its ground staff later for £2 10s.

On the poor, uncovered pitches of the day, Anderson achieved some remarkable bowling figures. In 1889 he took match figures of 10/127 against Nottinghamshire XI and 10/99 against MCC. In 1890 he took 7/13 in the first innings against Lincolnshire, 8/37 in the match against Northumberland, 4/52 against Yorkshire and 3/5 in

William 'Barney' Adamson			
Born: Gateshead, 1863			
Died: Gateshead, 1934(?)			
Batting			
M	I	NO	Runs
29	45	11	233
Ave	100		
6.85	158		
Bowling (no full analyses)			
O	Md	W	R
809.2+	251+	158	1,867
Ave	5wI	10wM	Ct
n/a	14	5	20
Best Performance			
8/18 *v.* Sussex, 1888			

the second innings, when Yorkshire wanted 29 to win. Durham captain Burgess Crosby promised Anderson £1 if he took three wickets. He dismissed Louis Hall, Edward Wainwright and George Hirst, but Crosby forgot to pay.

At the end of the last match of the season at York, Anderson asked for his money. Crosby said he was short and would pay up the next season. Anderson said: 'But you might be dead by then, captain.' Crosby said Anderson might be too. Anderson won the argument by saying: 'If I am dead, I wouldn't want it, but if you were dead, where would I go to get my £1?' Anderson would no doubt have spent the cash on nut brown ale, to which he was partial.

Bowling left arm with a high action, he took 12/97 against MCC, 14/76 against Northumberland in 1893 including the hat-trick, and 11/164 off 58.2 overs against Yorkshire II in an 1892 friendly.

Following more than a decade as North Durham professional, Anderson moved to Yorkshire, taking a Keighley club record 128 wickets at 7.63 in 1895.

Anderson, who became a good lawn bowler, still attended Durham's home games into the 1930s. With a little persuasion Hon. Secretary William Bell let the painter and decorator turned pioneering Durham professional in for free.

With more than 20 men named William Anderson dying in Gateshead each year in that era, it has proved impossible to find a date of death for 'Barney' Anderson.

Mohinder Armanath
RHB & RM, 1976-78

Already an experienced test player when he joined Durham, Mohinder Armanath used his Minor County spell to rebuild his batting after being dropped from India's team.

He regained his form, scoring five centuries in 28 innings for Durham, with bests of 115* against Staffordshire in 1976 and 117 against a Scottish XI in 1977. Games at obscure venues were something of a comedown for the Indian cricket blueblood. Paul Romaines recalled newcomer Armanath turning up an hour late for a county game, after driving to Stone in Warwickshire, rather than Staffordshire's Stone. However, 'Jimmy the Conquerer' took 6/28 in Staffordshire's 89 all out to set Durham on the way to the title. He scored 100* at Oxton, the first of his Durham centuries. In 1977 he headed the averages with 64.71. Armanath was known as a laid-back, westernised gentleman who enjoyed Durham so much he carried on playing for the county when he moved to the Lancashire leagues.

'A master stroke of signing', said captain Brian Lander; the boyishly good-looking 'Jimmy' led the Minor County averages in his first season, 1976, winning the Rhodes Trophy and helping Durham to its first Minor Counties title since 1930.

The first of Durham's professionals from the Indian subcontinent (though South Shields pro Cottari Subbanna [CS] Nayudu played in one friendly in 1956), Armanath followed New Zealander David O'Sullivan as part of the successful policy to introduce top overseas professionals into the Durham side.

Padmakar Shivalkar, Wasim Raja and 1995 signing Manoj Prabhakar, who was later banned from cricket for match fixing, followed. Indian left arm seamer Dhiranj Parsana took 60 wickets in 18 matches from 1976-82, but did not make Armanath's impact.

Armanath had a noble cricket pedigree as son of test player Lal (who scored 11 and four and took 1-27 and 0-66 in India's 1936 defeat at Ashbrooke) and brother of first-class cricketers Surinder and Rajinder. Later on during that 1936 tour, Lal swore at his captain, Maharajah Sir Vijay Vizianagram, after being dropped down the order against Minor Counties. Vizianagram sent him home, but Armanath's stance eventually helped end the domination of Indian cricket by the imperial element.

Mohinder Armanath was pro for South Shields in 1976 and Lowerhouse in the Lancashire League in 1977-78. Later Durham filled its overseas quota with Lance Cairns and Wasim Raja, so Armanath, who loved playing for Durham, accepted an approach from Wiltshire. He was the only Durham player to average over 50 post-war, and the only one apart from Wasim Raja to beat 40.

Mohinder Armanath			
Born: Patiala, India, 24 September 1950			
Batting			
M	I	NO	Runs
18	28	8	1,066
Ave	100	50	
53.30	3	5	
Bowling			
O	Md	R	W
268.2	75	642	34
Ave	5wI	10wM	Ct
18.88	1	0	14

Best Performances
117 v. Scottish XI, 1977
6/28 v. Staffordshire, 1976

In international cricket, Armanath was India's comeback man, scoring centuries on a recall to the Indian side three times. He had a sound technique, despite an unorthodox square-on stance. His batting was characterised by a fearless determination. Lander said Armanath was the finest player of spin he had seen, almost lying on the ball to ensure it didn't pass.

Ronald Aspinall
RHB & RFM, 1951-57

100 GREATS

Durham's best opening duo had much in common in their backgrounds, but little in their luck. Fast bowler Alec Coxon came north after his fiery temperament caused him to leave Yorkshire after the 1950 season. Coxon's opening partner, gentle giant Ron Aspinall, was also forced to look for alternative employment away from Headingley in 1951, because injury had ruined a possible England career.

Aspinall had taken 22/140 in two May fixtures against Somerset as recently as 1949, but hurt his Achilles tendon during a spell of 0/16 off nine overs in the next game against Worcestershire. He never played for Yorkshire with much effect again, leaving him top of the 1949 national averages with 30 wickets at 9.63.

His best years had been 1947 and 1948 (highlighted by dismissing Don Bradman), when Yorkshire captain Norman Yardley, who had discovered him playing services cricket in the Middle East during the war, said: 'I hope he will make an England player one day.' However, his exhausting bowling action led to strains, though at its best all he needed to take wickets was to bowl fast and straight.

A Durham City professional from 1951-56 (2572 runs and 527 wickets) and Gateshead Fell in 1957, Aspinall shredded club and Minor County batting orders in the early 1950s with his slowed down off cutters and off-breaks. He recombined effectively with Coxon, taking 6/84 against the 1952 Indians at Ashbrooke, helping give Durham a first innings lead of 146. However, against South Africa three years later he went for 126 off 16 overs at the same venue.

Coxon was something of a bad influence on Aspinall and the Tyke pair together could be mischievous. However, in one game at Keswick Aspinall angered Coxon by playing pitch and putt. It had rained so much on the way from the North-East to the Lakes that the bottom of a car, a Wolseley, driven by ex-captain Tom Coulson's son, Forster, had fallen out after going underwater in one of the dips on the Roman Wall road, drenching all-rounder Malcolm Scott. It was still

Ronald Aspinall
Born: Huddersfield, 26 October 1918
Died: Huddersfield, 16 August 1999
Also played for: Yorkshire

Batting

M	I	NO	Runs
59	77	9	1,238
Ave	100	50	
18.20	1	4	

Bowling

O	Md	R	W
1,459.3	387	3,766	185
Ave	5wI	10wM	Ct
20.35	11	2	35

Best Performances
101* v. Staffordshire, 1956
8/42 v. Cumberland and Westmorland, 1953

raining at Keswick, so big Ronnie and rugby player and occasional Durham CCC player Ken Land went to play pitch and putt. The rain stopped and play began, with cherry-faced Hon. Secretary Jack Iley having to replace the missing golfers. Irascible Coxon moved one off the seam, Cumberland's opener edged it and Iley dropped the chance at slip. Coxon turned the sky blue as Iley spotted Aspinall and Land sheepishly sneaking through Fitz Park gates. Iley started swearing, while the rest of the players fell about.

Laid-back Aspinall survived to head the Durham bowling averages in 1953 taking 37 wickets at 18.35. He also acted as a coach and groundsman in Durham, working as a joiner in the winters.

In 1958 and 1959, Aspinall coached at St Peter's School, York, where Yardley and Brian Sellers had been pupils. He was a Minor Counties and then an efficient first-class umpire from 1960-81. Wisden said he 'was dropped without much ceremony' just short of his official retirement.

Stephen Robert Atkinson
RHB & RM, 1972-89

As a leading professional performer with Chester-le-Street, Durham City and Shotley Bridge, and a Minor County player, Steve Atkinson bubbled beneath first-class level for most of the 1970s.

A footloose drama teacher, Atkinson played for The Hague and de Kievieten while working in Holland from 1982-84 and later in Hong Kong, but his biggest contribution came in 18 seasons for Durham.

The naturally gifted, tall and elegant 'Akkers' played a key role in the Durham success story of the 1970s and 1980s. In 1977 he scored 589 Championship runs, 695 in 1979, 574 in 1981, in 1982 he hit 505 runs at 50.5 and in 1983, 517 at 51.70, although in the Championship-winning year of 1981 he scored 341 at 21.31. The amateur opera singer, piano player and comedian's dressing room catchphrase was: 'Enjoy it lads – you could be down the pit.'

Opening against Yorkshire in the historic 1973 Gillette Cup win, Atkinson took a big chunk out of the victory target of 135, adding 58 with Russell Inglis.

Atkinson was much admired by his captain, Neil Riddell, who said he played brilliantly for 88 against Lancashire II at Chester-le-Street in 1979,

when set 207 in 38 minutes and 20 overs against test players Mick Malone and Paul Allott.

In the last Championship-winning season, 1984, on a wearing St Albans pitch (Atkinson often batted well when the chips were down), he scored 61 in Durham's second innings of 192/8 in the challenge match against Hertfordshire. A big match player, at Fenners in 1985 Atkinson set Durham towards a first English Estates Minor County one-day trophy in the third year of the competition. Opening, he hit the highest score in finals, 85, in Durham's 229/9. Durham bowled Dorset out for 129 to win by 100 runs. In 1985, Atkinson scored 483 runs at 37.15, second in the averages behind Riddell.

Full of wanderlust, Atkinson's teaching in Holland and Hong Kong led to two appearances in the ICC Trophy. He helped Holland to the 1986 ICC final after smashing 162 against Israel at Solihull and 107 against Hong Kong in the next game. Aged forty-one, the larger-than-life Atkinson played for Hong Kong in the 1993/94 Tournament. He always rated his fastish bowling, though his skill in this area is perhaps shown when he bowled a single over in his ICC career, conceding 37 runs. He was a good catcher at gully.

Stuart Wilkinson said: 'He was one of the most attractive batsmen I've ever seen.'

| Stephen Robert Atkinson |
| Born: Birtley, 8 December 1952 |

Batting

M	I	NO	Runs
139	237	20	6,959
Ave	100	50	
32.06	5	43	

Bowling

O	Md	R	W	Ct
15.3	3	64	0	96

Best Performance
155* v. Cheshire, 1982

Lance Cairns said: 'Along with Romaines, he was the clown of the side, a bubbly very, very talented guy who probably didn't do justice to himself. He could have gone to county cricket; he was a guy whose approach to the game I loved. He went out there and went after the bowling from the word go, didn't muck around, went for his shots. Sure enough he would give his wicket away at times, but his approach to the game was to get on top of the bowling and he'd score his runs quickly, which was a huge advantage.'

Arthur Whitelock Austin

RHB & WK, 1936-54

100 GREATS

| Arthur Whitelock Austin |
| Born: Stockton, 20 October 1908 |

Batting

M	I	NO	Runs
60	75	19	429
Ave	100	50	
7.66	67	62	

As a wicketkeeper, Arthur Austin played 15 seasons for Durham either side of the Second World War, but as an administrator he had a greater role to come.

Chairman of the club from 1975, Austin played a leading role in Durham achieving first-class status in 1992. In 1986 he was on the Durham sub-

committee looking at the issue and signed an official application letter in 1989 to the TCCB. Representing the past on the application video, Austin was surprised at the speed (within two years) that Durham became a first-class county.

The club elected the grand old man as its first patron that year and named its bar and bistro after him. In 1999, Austin celebrated his 90th birthday at Riverside. The directors of Durham CCC presented him with a bat signed by all the county wicketkeepers of 1992 and a print of Riverside, painted by one of his successors to the wicketkeeping gloves, Martin Speight.

From Stockton, the hometown of another dapper little man, John Walker, who invented the safety match, Austin lit up his debut in the win against India in 1936 by catching Maharajah Sir Vijay Vizianagram. 'There was the Maharajah, sitting down with two little servants, both no taller than four feet six inches, each putting a pad on for him. They soon had to take them off, because I caught him off Arnie Close for five,' he told Jack Bannister.

Stockton club player Austin, who also represented Durham at hockey, made his Championship debut in a tie with Northumberland in 1936 and was captain when David Townsend was unavailable in 1939.

After Dunkirk, Herbert Sutcliffe asked Austin to bring a team to his Garrison at Catterick, when the Abe Waddington-like Freddie Herbert dismissed the first three of a side including Sutcliffe, Hutton and Verity in the first five overs.

His batting, rarely a feature, impressed in 1951 when he saw Durham home to a two-wicket win at Stone against Staffordshire.

Exceptional standing up, particularly in making legside stumpings, Austin was the first Durham wicketkeeper to make seven dismissals in a match twice, with five catches and 2 stumpings against Yorkshire II in 1948, and four catches and three stumpings against Northumberland the following year. Only Johnny Common had dismissed seven before.

Austin, always immaculately dapper and as smart as a carrot on and off the field, became a watchword for service at the county. He wore a cravat, recalling the old amateur days, and worked as a cheesemaker for his father's firm, which he later sold to Wensleydale Cheeses.

Durham appointed Austin Hon. Secretary in 1969, following two former captains, Cecil Ferens and Ernest Proud in the role. He was an important fundraiser and sponsorship finder over the years, still appearing at Durham functions into his nineties.

Harry John Bailey
RHB & LM, 1961-71

Harry John Bailey
Born: West Hartlepool, 23 April 1940

Batting

M	I	NO	Runs
99	128	11	2,565
Ave	100	50	
21.91	2	11	

Bowling

O	Md	R	W
742.3	158	2,150	82
Ave	5wI	10wM	Ct
26.21	1	0	41

Best Performances
108 v. Staffordshire, 1967
6/41 v. Staffordshire, 1968

From a cricket (and legal) family, John Bailey's finest hour for Durham was in the 1967 GC match against Nottinghamshire at Chester-le-Street.

Bailey's left arm medium bowled three of Notts' top four, captain Norman Hill, Roy Swetman and

Mike Smedley, in an analysis of 12-4-37-3. Coming in (behind his brother David) at 101/4, chasing 192 to win, his 30 took Durham to the brink of what would have been the first win by a Minor County over first-class opposition in the competition. However, Bailey was run out at 180 in the last over and Durham lost by 11 runs. He won the Man of the Match award and had some success in a subsequent GC tie with 2/24 against Worcestershire in 1968 and for the Minor Counties against the tourists from 1966-69. His elegant batting brought 506 runs at 33.71 in 1967, his best season.

After filling in as skipper in Don Hardy's absence in 1966 and 1967, he captained Durham for four seasons (1968-71) progressing from ninth to nineteenth, to tenth then second place. In 1968, Durham failed to qualify for the 1969 GC, and the same thing happened in the following two seasons. In 1969, Durham won just a single game, and Bailey averaged 9.10 with the bat. In 1971 Bailey could only play twice because of injury, with Russell Inglis taking the captaincy.

Bailey played for the School XI at Malvern in the late 1950s, and was a West Hartlepool player when he made 101 in an innings win against

Cumberland at Keswick in 1962 during his second season with Durham. He came in at No.7 with the score 89/5, and took Durham to 301/9 declared to set up the win. That year he scored 412 runs at 29.24, winning his cap.

His father, solicitor Harry Ernest Bailey played five games for the county from 1938-40 and was a committee member from 1953. He became Hon. Secretary in 1975, succeeding Arthur Austin. Harry Bailey died in 1977. John's brother David played for Malvern School, West Hartlepool and Durham from 1961-67, scoring 519 runs in 1966 and 1,010 in his 21-game Durham career. He moved to Lancashire, then played for Cheshire from 1982 and captained Minor Counties. John Bailey later became District Judge for Teesside and Darlington, and his son James carried on the family cricket tradition by working as a Durham CCC marketing executive.

Philip Bainbridge
RHB & RM, 1992-96

100 GREATS

Philip Bainbridge			
Born: Stoke-on-Trent, 16 April 1958			
Also played for: Gloucestershire			

Batting

M	I	NO	Runs
67	115	13	3,354
Ave	100	50	
32.88	2	25	

Bowling

O	Md	R	W
975.3	208	3,109	76
Ave	5wI	10wM	Ct
40.90	3	0	39

Best Performances
150* v. Essex, 1993
5/53 v. Yorkshire, 1993

Simon Hughes wondered how indestructible Phil Bainbridge's 'dribbly assortment of slow swingers and loopy slower balls' were so effective and how he was able to bat 'on four hours sleep and a bloodstream that was 40 percent proof.'

Bainbridge came to Durham in 1991 following 14 seasons and over 12,000 first-class runs and 250 wickets for Gloucestershire, where he and David Graveney shared the same final game

Useful on difficult pitches with the bat and at keeping control in one-day games with his inswing, Bainbridge had been Graveney's vice-captain at Gloucestershire. Graveney said Bainbridge was a 'captain's player, and one I knew would do the job for Durham.'

He had turned down a Gloucestershire contract for 1991 to concentrate on his corporate hospitality sports tour business, so Durham had to ask the TCCB for permission to sign him. It proved a worthwhile decision.

Bainbridge's experience with Durham in 1991 helped Graveney when he became Durham's first first-class captain in 1992. Bainbridge, who also played as pro for Northern League winners Leyland, scored 512 runs at 32.00 and took 21 wickets at 29.19 in 1991, and Graveney worried if he could effectively return to the county game.

He was a success, coming second in the averages behind Dean Jones with 923 runs at 43.95, though he took just 14 wickets at 40.64.

In 1993, the ever-competitive Bainbridge shone in a miserable Championship season. He topped the batting and bowling averages, earning him the Durham Player of the Year award.

The popular 'Bains' succeeded Graveney as Durham

captain in 1994, but it badly affected his batting and he handed on to Mike Roseberry for 1995. A lifelong cricket pro, Bainbridge worried more than most about what he would do when his playing days were over.

His fluent stroke play returned on occasion in 1996 after he scored just four first-class runs and took one wicket in 1995.

Bainbridge, who played for four second XIs in 1976 (Gloucestershire, Derbyshire, Northamptonshire, Warwickshire) often found himself in Durham's seconds in 1995 and 1996, so the former Young England player (*v.* Australia 1977), who was one of Wisden's five players of the year in 1985, retired to the sports hospitality business that suited his personality so well.

100 GREATS

Henry Davey Bell
RHB, 1944-62

Henry Davey Bell			
Born: Castletown, 14 October 1924			

Batting

M	I	NO	Runs
26.48	152	11	3,735
Ave	100	50	
26.48	4	17	

Bowling

O	Md	R	W	Ct
18.2	1	85	1	48

Best Performance
186 *v.* Lancashire II, 1960

B est known as a right half with Middlesbrough FC, with his name easily slipping off the tongue of adoring fans, Harry Bell often carried the Durham batting in the 1950s, to lesser acclaim but equal personal satisfaction.

Durham batsman Alan Parnaby 'took me under his wing' at Ashbrooke, said Bell, whose hopes of a first-class contract with Somerset or Middlesex were dashed by the war.

Bell's fellow Boro footballer George Dews played for Worcestershire, but later it was more difficult to combine cricket and football. Malcolm Tate was sacked by Darlington FC when the 1962 season ran into the cricket season, and scruffy fast bowler Alan Ramage, who played for Middlesbrough FC and Yorkshire CC, didn't even seem to have time to wash his whites. Amateurs Ernest Proud, who played amateur football internationals, and Graham Doggart who won a full international cap in combining the sports, found it easier.

Debonair and elegant, Bell brought a toughness to the Durham side with his professional football ethic. An athletic example in the field, Bell gave the Durham lads focus – a focus he showed by trying just as hard in a Sunday benefit game as in the football league.

'I didn't get a holiday, but it worked well, because as soon as I was playing the last few matches for Middlesbrough I was going into the nets at night,' Bell said.

Compact and of medium height, Bell could murder mediocre bowling and could always judge opponents' weaknesses. In 1951, the free-scoring opener scored Durham's only century of the season, 104* in 95 minutes in the nine wicket win over Cheshire at Wallasey. Durham, boosted by Ron Aspinall and Alec Coxon, finished fourth in the Championship, with Bell scoring 316 runs at 35.11. In 1952, he established an opening partnership record with Jackie Keeler of 215, against Yorkshire II. He also hit a NYSD League record five centuries that year, after moving from Crook to Middlesbrough, and the framed memento Boro CC gave him filled him with pride into late life. He beat David Townsend's record of four centuries in his last innings of the season before returning to Ayresome

Henry Davey Bell

continued

Park. Bell was a North-East sporting hero, recognised wherever he went. 'I didn't mind that – it was alright,' he said. He enjoyed the atmosphere of Middlesbrough FC and Durham CCC. 'It was a good team spirit in those days at Durham. It was like the football at Middlesbrough. We had a good side.' With George Hardwick, Wilf Mannion and Bell's best friend, Mickey Fenton, Boro's side did have some classic names, but Bell said Bill Proud ('a heavyweight'), Alec Coxon ('a funny lad, typical Yorkshireman') and Ron Aspinall made his summers as fulfilling as his winters.

In 1955, his best season for Durham CCC, he hit 547 runs at 42.07, combining well with Keeler to add 153 against Yorkshire II as the side finished third under new captain Don Hardy.

In 1956 he topped the averages with 30.23 including the team's season high, 90 in the win against Northumberland at Jesmond. In 1958 he declined to 259 runs at 21.58, when again no Durham player scored a century. In 1960 he put on 182 with Russell Inglis, going on to his career best, 186, Durham's then highest innings behind Edgar Elliot's two double-centuries.

His final appearance for the county, his 100th, came aged 37 in the last Championship game of 1962, when he top scored with 63 in the draw against Lancashire II.

Bell later became a brewery sales representative with William Younger, then a brewery area manager, fixing people up with pubs. He gave up golf when 78, after over 60 years of sporting endeavour.

Melvyn Morris Betts — 100 GREATS

RHB & RFM, 1993-2000

Melvyn Morris Betts

Born: Durham, 26 March 1975
Also played for: Warwickshire, England A, Middlesex

Batting

M	I	NO	Runs
67	104	23	956
Ave	100	50	
11.80	0	2	

Bowling

O	Md	R	W
1,811.5	370	6,186	223
Ave	5wl	10wM	Ct
27.73	10	2	21

Best Performances
57* v. Sussex, 1996 (partnering David Cox in a Durham 10th-wicket record of 103)
9/64 v. Northamptonshire, 1997 (Durham record)

Melvyn Betts is Durham's 'one that got away'. After decades of losing its best players to first-class counties, Betts, possibly the Durham player with most potential, left for Warwickshire for the 2001 season.

Club Chairman Bill Midgley said: 'It is particularly disappointing that a young player in whom the Club has invested a great deal of time and money in his development has chosen to pursue his career elsewhere. It is especially sad after Durham

had offered him significantly improved terms.'

Betts said: 'Warwickshire have been one of the most successful clubs over the last ten years. It's the chance to play at a Test match ground and they have a good coach in Bob Woolmer. I felt that my career had come to a bit of a standstill at Durham. I haven't enjoyed my cricket over the last couple of years and hopefully I can now look forward to reporting back for pre-season training instead of going through the same old routine.'

Betts accepted a lucrative offer (perhaps double what Durham could muster), and the Sacriston through-and-through, rather complex, neurotic character, moved to the relatively successful Warwickshire team. He took a match-winning 5/22 at Edgbaston on his Warwickshire debut against Durham. Ironically, by the end of 2003, Betts' move backfired as Warwickshire, to save money, did not renew his contract.

Betts' father, also Melvyn, and uncle played for Sacriston. The unworldly teenager toured Sri Lanka with England Under-19s in 1993/94 and played against India in 1994. He missed six weeks of 1995 with an Achilles injury, finishing with 17 wickets at 50.17, having played one first-class game in 1993, taking 1/19.

Betts' career highlight came in 1997 despite an early setback of a broken ankle. He took 9/64 and 13/143 in the match; Durham drew, but the dream attack of Betts and Simon Brown gelled at last.

However, the home grown left-hand/right-hand opening pair's partnership did not endure.

Betts won his cap in 1998 with 44 championship wickets at 21.45, (he took 43 at 21.83 in 1997) but took a frustrating 20 wickets at 29.15 in 1999. He boiled over twice, earning one fine.

Betts' whippy, fast outswing won him selection for the 1998/99 England 'A' tour to South Africa, but a torn groin muscle sustained bowling his fourth ball of the innings against Glamorgan in August 1998 ruined his trip.

Betts came back in 2000, with 44 Championship wickets at 18.90 including 7/30 against Derbyshire in an innings win at Darlington.

After Betts left, the Durham dream of a home-produced side seemed shattered, but by May 2002 ten Durham-born lads, all under 28, (plus Martin Love) made up the team against Gloucestershire at Chester-le-Street.

Betts moved to Middlesex for the 2004 season.

100 GREATS

Kenneth David Biddulph
RHB & RFM, 1962-72

Ken Biddulph
Born: Chingford, 29 May 1932
Died: 7 January 2003, Stroud
Also played for: Somerset

Batting

M	I	NO	Runs
82	71	33	353
Ave	100	50	
9.28	0	0	

Bowling

O	Md	R	W
2,266.5	732	5,390	300
Ave	5wl	10wM	Ct
17.96	17	3	19

Best Performance
8/47 *v.* Staffordshire, 1964

A player who devoted his life to cricket, Ken Biddulph was coaching cricket on the day he died.

He contributed to Somerset's 1958 third place in the Championship. Even Ian Botham, Viv Richards and Joel Garner could not better that effort. Biddulph never fully established himself at Somerset, taking 270 wickets in seven seasons

before heading north. He had escaped a career in the Borough Treasurer's Department in Chingford via a London Evening News scheme coached by Alf Gover. David Foot said Somerset's Harold Gimblett arranged a two-year contract, which led to Biddulph's seven first-class years.

'Biddy,' who Trevor Bailey described as a 'bag of bones', played for Durham for eight seasons with considerable success, and in 1963 he topped the averages, taking 61 wickets at 13. In his first season, 1962, he combined well with Stuart Young, taking 38 wickets at 18.34. In 1964 the 6ft 4ins, fair-haired brisk seamer took 13/94 against Staffordshire (8/47 and 5/47) to help win the match by nine wickets.

The professional for Hartlepool, Sunderland, Whitburn and Boldon, who later ran a pub, was known to be a gentleman as a player and as a coach, who bowled big inswingers and taught many young players, including Test player Ken Palmer, the craft. He was renowned for his patience with children (he was coach at Wycliffe College) and used to stay in the nets until dark with anyone who matched his enthusiasm for the game.

Bath author Stephen Chalke, who was inspired to become a cricket writer by his friendship with Biddulph, made a card listing some of the players Biddulph dismissed, who included Colin Cowdrey, John Edrich, Peter May and Tom Graveney.

'Those were the days you bowled at the wickets, especially on the green 'uns at Taunton,' said wicketkeeper Bobby Cole, Biddulph's long-time friend. Chalke also told the story of Bill Alley deciding Biddulph's bat was too good for the tailender. The ageless Aussie scored 3,000 runs using it in 1961, while Biddulph used an old one of Alley's.

Former Durham all-rounder Jack Watson said Biddulph and Stuart Young 'brilliantly' added six yards to his run in a game against Yorkshire II at Feethams in which Yorkshire needed 40-odd to win in 90 minutes. Durham almost drew, but Yorkshire sent someone in to run out Geoff Boycott.

As scorer Brian Hunt said: 'Kenny loved playing for Durham, gave his all in every match, never said a bad word against a soul.'

Peter Cresswell Birtwisle

RHB & RM, 1965-84

Like Geoffrey Boycott's hundredth hundred at Headingley in the 1977 Ashes series, Peter Birtwisle also chose a centenary to score a landmark century. In 1982, on his 100th Durham appearance, he hit his maiden century for the county, 101 against Cheshire at Hartlepool – it was to be his sole three figure score for the county he served for 20 years.

Birtwisle was a steady middle order batsman, with career highlights including a score of 59 against Northants, which took Durham close to victory in the 1977 Gillette Cup first round. In his first season, 1965, the technically correct Birtwisle scored 48; adding 103 with captain Don Hardy in the quest for first innings points against Staffordshire. However, Durham stuttered and lost its last four wickets for 25 runs. Birtwisle's career stuttered too and it was not until 1974 that he made a major impact, scoring more than 300 runs to be second to Steve Greensword in aggregates for the season.

Birtwisle's innings of 79 against Cheshire in the 1976 Championship-winning season was crucial. In 1977, he averaged more than 30 and he also contributed steadily to the Championship-winning teams of the 1980s. He played for Worcestershire II and Minor Counties East. The Sunderland club stalwart moved to Durham City in 1982.

His son Simon Birtwisle played for Durham Cricket Board, Northumberland and Bradford/ Leeds UCCE. 'Birty' was well schooled by Alec Coxon as a young player at Sunderland and in turn passed on his

Peter Cresswell Birtwisle			
Born: Sunderland, 2 August 1946			
Also played for: Minor Counties			
Batting			
M	I	NO	Runs
108	153	30	3,122
Ave	100	50	
25.38	1	12	
Bowling			
O	Md	R	W
21	8	45	11.25
Ave	Ct		
11.25	70		
Best Performance			
101 v. Cheshire, 1982			

knowledge to son Simon.

A teacher turned optician, Birtwisle wasn't a Durham regular, partly because of work commitments, but when he played he was 'a dasher, always in a hurry', said Lance Cairns. 'He didn't muck around and play himself in for an hour; he liked to play his shots. He was attractive to watch. If you had a toff in your side, he was the toff. Maybe he thought he was a little bit better educated. Riddell tried to talk posh, though he wasn't, but Birty had a bit of background about him.'

David Clarence Boon

RHB & OB, 1997-99

David Clarence Boon
Born: Launceston, Tasmania, 29 December 1960
Also played for: Tasmania, Australia

Batting

M	I	NO	Runs
50	86	9	3,007
Ave	100	50	
39.05	7	20	

Bowling

O	Md	R	W
45	12	163	4
Ave	Ct		
40.75	39		

Best Performance
139* v. Yorkshire, 1998

The giddiness of first-class status had faded when David Boon took the Durham captaincy in 1997. A coup for Durham's management after four years of modest returns from its captains, David Graveney, Phil Bainbridge, Mike Roseberry and Nick Speak and imports Sherwin Campbell, Anderson Cummins and Manoj Prabhakar, Boon was Durham's big hope to re-swell interest in the county's cricket.

Boon had already written two autobiographies, 1993's *In the Firing Line* and 1996's *Under the Southern Cross*; he was a popular Australian close to retirement.

Spool forward to September 1999: 'I've enjoyed every one of my 21 years in first-class cricket and to end like this is like the icing on the cake,' said Boon. Durham had won promotion against the odds for the first year of the twin division championship and Boon's job was done.

Loyal to his team and people he knew, Boon was a gentleman off the field whose giggly, full-of-fun nature was opposite to his combative nature on it. Openly driven by the fear of failure, proud of the middle name of Clarence he inherited from his father, Boon still can make a roomful stop talking just by walking in, such is his legendary reputation in cricket.

Tasmanian Boon, with his mullet haircut, yard-brush moustache and flared trousers even drew mockery from notoriously style-free Kiwi Richard Hadlee, but Boon's pride, not his fashion mattered to Durham's fans.

Boon's signing was a risk. He'd ended the season with Tasmania in 1996 with first ball duck, and aged 36, it could have been a season too far for the 107-test veteran.

From eighteenth and last in 1996, Durham rose a single place in the Championship and Sunday League in 1997, though Boon told Wisden: 'The improvement is in the way we have competed in terms of commitment, demeanour and attitude. There wasn't a county we played against who didn't remark on the vast improvement in the team.'

The 5ft 7in captain of perennial Sheffield Shield strugglers Tasmania knew how to build a side from raw, and showed faith in Paul Collingwood and Melvyn Betts, while John Morris and new boy Jonathan Lewis prospered.

In 1998, Durham rose to second in the table by early June and although Boon's side tailed off to fourteenth, he added another year to his contract, telling Wisden: 'The team spirit here is fantastic. I can't see it being better anywhere else.'

Boon was always worth more than his modest returns of 981 Championship runs at 37.73 in 1997, 953 at 39.70 in 1998, and 839 at 33.56 in 1999, when Durham exceeded pundits' expectations after a dreadful start. 'As the Championship scrap reached its finale, Boon showed his true fighting qualities', said Wisden. The country's leading fast bowling attack (Simon Brown, Stephen Harmison, Neil

David Clarence Boon
continued

Killeen, John Wood and Betts) helped the side to six wins with 241 wickets between them. After being bottom in July, Durham surged to the top eight, six higher than its previous best in 1998. The man who holds the tinnie record for an Australia to England flight and who had been in the 1987 World Cup winning side became a Durham hero.

However, even as Boon left, not everything was well. Betts was disillusioned; the team had no effective spinner or all-rounder and an untried overseas player in Simon Katich. Significantly, Durham had no clear captain figure, though the team supported Nick Speak's selection. By midway through 2000, the crowd were crying out for Boon's return, testament to his success and influence in the three seasons that regenerated Durham.

Ian Terence Botham

RHB & RFM, 1992-93

Ian Terence Botham
Born: Heswall, 24 November 1956
Also played for: Somerset, England, Worcestershire, Queensland

Batting

M	I	NO	Runs
25	40	3	1,121
Ave	100	50	
30.29	2	7	

Bowling

O	Md	R	W
507.5	108	1,599	39
Ave	5wI	10wM	Ct
41.00	0	0	15

Best Performances
105 v. Leicestershire, 1992 (Durham debut)
4/11 v. Glamorgan, 1993

Ian Botham complained with vitriol about his time at Durham in his 1994 autobiography *Don't Tell Kath*. Yet Botham often did what he pleased during his season and a half at the county, earning plenty of cash and rewarding Durham reciprocally with a kick-start of publicity and popularity.

Botham, England's greatest post-war cricketer, was Durham captain David Graveney and Director of Cricket Geoff Cook's star signing for the county's inaugural first-class season. Botham's signing gave Durham legitimacy as a force in English cricket.

However, even before he'd moved north (albeit within commuting distance of his Richmondshire home), Botham found fuel for any later grudge. Chairman Don Robson, backer Matty Roseberry and a sponsor offered him the captaincy, Botham said. Cook told Botham it was already Graveney's.

After the January 1992 World Cup in New Zealand and Australia, Botham sought to rejuvenate his playing life at his third county. Cook offered Simon Hughes £15,000 a year – Botham

must have been on double that. Graveney said: 'My view was that the commercial benefit of signing someone of Ian's status was too big to pass up.'

England's selectors, hoping for a remembrance of things past, gave Botham more international chances against Pakistan in 1992 after he briefly prospered for Durham.

Botham was getting results more on reputation and guile than anything else and it couldn't last. Dean Jones said: 'Blimey, this man's arse is kissed innit?' It was fun for a while.

Simon Hughes said: 'Had a pint of Castle Eden in the Dun Cow. Botham and Richards said they'd join us, but disappeared into a back room of the pavilion and locked the door. What they were doing there your guess is as good as mine.' Expectations were high and Botham scored a century against Leicestershire, but averaged 41.65 for his 26 first-class wickets. One-dayers now suited his limited fitness and concentration and he took 20 one-day wickets and scored 602 runs, with six fifties in 16 innings.

Botham was over the hill when he arrived at Durham, but could still turn it on in a winning cause. Always the rebel, he still hated authority, but loved his friends. Botham used to spend thousands on barbeques for his new Durham cricket mates. They, in turn, would do anything for him, including caddying – Botham was impossible to argue with.

Botham's last test was against Pakistan in 1992, when he took 0/52 off 19 overs, and did not bat. There was no play on the first day and two deliveries on the next and angry spectators didn't get their money back, which prompted a change in the rules. Pakistan, with 141/8, won the match by two wickets. Chris Lewis, one of many all-rounders to be called the new Botham, took 3/34. Botham didn't bowl in the second innings, but took two catches to equal Cowdrey's record of 120, one of them to remove Moin Khan off Phil DeFreitas, yet another new Botham. For the next Test the selectors replaced Botham, Allan Lamb (with whom Botham was doing speaking tours) and DeFreitas with Mike Atherton, David Gower and Tim Munton.

Botham had one last cricket wish – to be selected for the 1993 Ashes series. It did not happen. He had a plan to retire in September 1993. His fitness and patience did not last that long.

England captain Graham Gooch said: 'It was a bit sad in the end at Durham seeing him bowl those diddly-doddlers and getting carted all over the ground.' Durham keeper Chris Scott said on Botham's retirement, after an unsuccessful swan-song for Durham against the Aussies: 'That's part of my childhood gone.'

Botham knew too he was over the hill: 'I'm like a battered old Escort, you might find one panel that's original,' he said, complaining that after ten operations it took five minutes for him to get out of bed. Botham's gripe was that Roseberry had tried to involve him in a coup against Robson, as a 'stool pigeon' in Botham's words. 'The petty-mindedness of the club appalled me', Botham, a man for large gestures, said.

Botham became a media pundit. He'd said of Somerset: 'I hope they don't win anything for 100 years', and showed a similar negativity towards Durham. Later he made up with the county where he made his name; and in time will surely do so with Durham.

Robert Bousfield

RHB & RM/OB, 1887-1906

Robert Bousfield			
Born: Etherley, 28 September 1868			
Died: Gosforth, 29 April 1929			

Batting

M	I	NO	Runs
89	143	5	3,066
Ave	100	50	
22.21	4	10	

Bowling

O	Md	R	W
207.3	52	580	19
Ave	Ct		
30.52	46		

Best Performance
160 v. Northamptonshire, 1898

Bob Bousfield began and ended his cricket at King James I Grammar School in Bishop Auckland, where he was a pupil and later headmaster.

A precocious cricketer, he scored 40 out of 55 and took 10 wickets for the school against the Church Institute (Bousfield was very religious, though he was competitive on the field, befitting the Victorian trend for muscular Christianity) in 1884, the year before his Bishop Auckland debut, when he played with his father Robert Robson Bousfield.

In 1887, at 18, Bousfield scored 167 for Bishops against Middlesbrough. At Durham University he hit 494 runs as a freshman, including a remarkable 245* out of 442-8 in a match at Ashbrooke.

The stylish, free-scoring driver and useful medium pacer, who was sometimes reluctant to bowl, played for the University until 1891, when he graduated with an MA. In 1892/93 he played for Barnard Castle where he was assistant headmaster of the County School. He played for North East County School from 1884-96.

In 1897 he was appointed head at King James' and he represented Bishop Auckland at cricket and football, appearing as a fullback in the 1899/1900 Amateur Cup winning team against Lowestoft Town. He was also a prodigious runscorer for Durham at this time, with 718 in 1899, which would have broken Edgar Elliot's Durham record from the previous season, had Elliot not done it himself, with 738.

Bousfield captained Bishop Auckland CC from 1898-1905 and Durham in 1897. He scored 12 centuries for Bishops prior to it joining the NYSD League, and six more after 1905. He also bowled effective medium fast, but was generally reluctant to put himself on.

The lifelong gentleman servant of sport and education and epitome of the Bishop Auckland sportsman, he scored 3,103 runs in seven seasons in the League before retiring in 1913, playing occasionally until 1923.

Col. Sir Thomas Andrews Bradford DSO ——————— 100
LHB, 1909-14

Tommie Bradford began his great career of service to Durham on the cricket pitch. He was awarded a DSO in the First World War, serving as Commander of D Company of the 8th Battalion the Durham Light Infantry, whose HQ was at Birtley. He was the only one of four brothers (one of whom, Roland, won the Victoria Cross) to survive the war.

Bradford was knighted in 1939 for public service to his beloved Durham. He acted as Deputy-General of the county to Lord Londonderry, won an honorary doctorate (of civil law) from Durham University where he was Hon. Treasurer and was High Sheriff of the county in 1942.

From a service background and an education at the Royal Naval College in Kent, Bradford made a Gilbert Jessop-like 207* in 90 minutes for Chester-le-Street against Philadelphia in 1909, the season when he made his county debut.

He shared a county record fourth wicket stand of 250 with Cecil Brooks against Cheshire in 1910 and scored two centuries in 1911 and one in 1912, with only Elliot making more.

Bradford scored 377 runs at 53.85 in four games in 1911, combining well with Dick Harrison, who hit 783 at 43.50.

The powerful, attractive left-hander made 249 in 1912, playing only five innings due to military commitments. He was occasionally captain when Proud was unavailable. He also played as a county rugby forward from 1911-13.

Col. Sir Thomas Andrews Bradford DSO			
Born: Witton Park, 23 March 1886			
Died: Durham City, 29 December 1966			
Batting			
M	I	NO	Runs
25	41	3	1,519
Ave	100	50	
39.97	4	8	
Bowling			
O	Md	R	W	Ct
1	0	2	0	11
Best Performance			
168 v. Cheshire, 1910			

The 1915 county committee report congratulated Captain T.A. Bradford, Durham Light Infantry Territorial Force, on his award of DSO for bravery on the field. He was twice mentioned in dispatches at Ypres.

The county named Bradford vice-captain for 1919, but he did not play. The JP, Conservative candidate for Seaham (1922) and Durham (1923) and Sacriston colliery director lived at Whitesmocks near Durham where he enjoyed shooting on the moors.

Poignantly, Bradford named his son, born in 1920, George James Roland after his late brothers.

Hubert Brooks ——————————————————————— 100
RHB/RLB, 1906-29

Born in Darlington, Bertie Brooks, from an affluent background, spent most of his life in Sunderland, where he and middle brother Cecil were mainstays of the club side in the first part of the twentieth century. They, and another brother, Arnold, attended Mount Oswald public school in Scarborough and played cricket for Sunderland, Bertie from 1904-36.

Hubert Brooks

Born: Darlington, 1886
Died: Sunderland, 31 January 1967

Batting

M	I	NO	Runs
121	193	13	3,319
Ave	100	50	
18.43	2	11	

Bowling

O	Md	R	W
433.4	47	1,699	81
Ave	5wI	10wM	Ct
20.97	2	0	32

Best Performances
123 v. Northumberland, 1922
5/19 v. Lancashire II, 1922

At the club Bertie Brooks scored over 10,000 runs and took 397 wickets. He was a studied, well-schooled batsman, who made his runs against bowlers such as England's Sidney Barnes and George Thompson in the Minor Counties competition. Against Barnes' Staffordshire Brooks showed his worth by scoring 22 out of 45 and 77 in the second innings at Carley Hill in 1910.

'His technique was cultured; a look of caution mixed with confidence, but withal, serenity. His cover driving and strokes behind the wicket were eloquent with grace and skill always designed to beat the fielders, and he exploited a push stroke off his legs to the on, which produced many runs,' said D.G. Greig in the history of Sunderland cricket.

Brooks helped fill the gap left by Edgar Elliot at Sunderland and Durham, passing 500 runs a season six times for the club between 1909-21. He played for Durham every year from 1906-29, except for 1909 and 1920, when he was still in HM Forces.

He hit 123 against Northumberland and 111 against Yorkshire in 1922, his best year, when he scored 477 runs at 28.05 in all for the county.

In 1927, his stand of 195 for the ninth wicket with Jack Cook held New Zealand up in its march to a 10 wicket win.

Brooks was Durham's captain from 1924-28, after Tom Kinch. He took the county from twentieth in his first year to first in 1926, fourth in 1927 and third in 1928, when, aged 42, he passed the captaincy on to Cecil Ferens.

100 GREATS

Simon John Emmerson Brown
RHB & LFM, 1992-2002

Sunderland electrician Simon Brown failed to make the professional county cricket grade in four seasons with Northants. He returned home to Durham in 1991 with thoughts of giving the game up.

The Boldon CC professional had toured Sri Lanka with England Young Cricketers in 1987 and played in the Australia World Youth Cup in 1987/88 but had made little progress afterwards, lacking 'one-to-one coaching and practice, rather than churning it out daily,' said David Graveney. 'I remember seeing him bowl... against Norfolk at the end of the 1991 season, and I saw enough of his action and movement of the ball to know that he was a bowler who could swing the ball and bowl aggressively. I thought then he would cope with regular first-class cricket.'

Brown nearly gave the game up before his 31 wickets in 1991 won him a two-year contract for 1992, when he led Durham's attack, taking 56 Championship wickets at 32.98. He carried the attack with performances such as his 7/105 against Kent at Canterbury.

Simon John Emmerson Brown
continued

Brown proved to be a consistent wicket-taker for England's youngest county side but perhaps paid the penalty, certainly in the county's early years, for having to carry an attack comprising novices and ageing veterans. But when the ball swung he could be a handful, moving it late and picking up a lot of lbws and bowleds.

In 1996 he won a test call-up, becoming the first homegrown Durham CCC player to play a Test. With his tenth ball, Brown dismissed Pakistan opener Aamer Sohail lbw, but the Lord's Test was Brown's first and last. Skinny, lugubrious, fond of a pint and moustachioed, 'Chubby' Brown said: 'I would have liked more caps, of course, but look what happened to other left-armers like Mike Smith of Gloucestershire – one cap and then that's it. Don't know why really.'

Brown maintained his flick hairstyle and moustache almost into the 21st century, but when he grew a beard and cut his hair, like Samson, his powers faded.

Brown was awarded a benefit year in 2001 by Durham as he approached his 500th first-class wicket.

Brown's career took off after he married in 1992. Durham supporters voted him player of the year in 1992, and he won Durham player of the year in 1994. Once offered a basketball scholarship in the US, 6ft 3in Brown was consistent throughout the 1990s, except from 1993, when his 37 Championship wickets cost 45.59. But all was not lost as he took a then career best 7/70 against the Australians at Durham, to give a first innings lead of 164, enabling Graveney to enforce Durham's first first-class era follow-on. The match ended as a draw, with Ian Botham keeping wicket without pads or gloves in the final over of his final first-class game.

As the big names fell away, John Lever fan Brown became Durham's star, taking 50 wickets in a season seven times, with a best of 79 in 1996 when he captained some games after Nick Speak lost his place.

In 1997 Durham die-hard Brown took 57

Simon John Emmerson Brown			
Born: Cleadon, 29 June 1969			
Also played for: Northamptonshire, England			

Batting

M	I	NO	Runs
141	205	65	1,715
Ave	100	50	
12.25	0	2	

Bowling

O	Md	R	W
4,414.2	845	14,664	518
Ave	5wI	10wM	Ct
28.31	36	2	35

Best Performances
69 *v.* Leicestershire, 1994
7/51 *v.* Lancashire, 2000

wickets at 29.24. This included match figures of 6/35 off 26.4 overs in the May win over Surrey and a career best 7/51 in the next game, which Lancashire won by 141 runs. He also took 10/141 *v.* Leicestershire. Uncharacteristically, this was the last game of the season (Brown usually faded due to fatigue). Characteristically, Durham lost (it hadn't won away in two seasons.)

In 2000, he took his 500th first-class wicket, Steve Stubbings of Derbyshire caught by Martin Speight.

His 2001 and 2002 seasons were ruined by injury and Durham released him after 2002. He later worked for Northern Rock Building Society, a county sponsor, and played for Sunderland.

His Durham records include most first-class appearances (141), most first-class wickets (518), a BHC best of 6-30 *v.* Northants at Chester le Street in 1997 and a ninth wicket record of 127, with David Ligertwood against Surrey at Stockton in 1996. Captain Jon Lewis, all-rounder Paul Collingwood and fast bowler Stephen Harmison all said Brown should be in the top five of any list of Durham greats.

Alan James Burridge
LHB & RM, 1961-72

An unusual cricket career path took much-travelled left-handed middle order batsman Alan Burridge from Wearmouth to St John's Wood via sides as diverse as Penrith, Lincolnshire and Enfield.

So dangerous was he that George Crawford said Burridge used to hit the ball as hard as Botham or Andrew Flintoff. The tall, gangly player was light around the field and confident in everything he tried,

Alan James Burridge
Born: Sunderland, 8 October 1936
Also played for: Hertfordshire, Minor Counties

Batting

M	I	NO	Runs
95	142	17	3,745
Ave	100	50	
29.96	3	22	

Bowling

O	Md	R	W
2.1	1	1	2
Ave	Ct		
0.50	92		

Best Performance
126* v. Lancashire II, 1961

'Budgie' hit the Minor County scene in 1961 with 308 runs at 38.50. Burridge (126*), aged 24, combined with Crawford (102*) to add 223 against Lancashire II, Durham's second highest fourth wicket partnership. He made few big scores but, with Russell Inglis, John Bailey, George March and Charlie Lamb, formed a top order that kept standards high prior to the GC breakthroughs and Championship wins of the 1970s and 1980s. Burridge scored centuries for Durham in his first and last seasons, with one in between, against Northumberland in 1967. Playing for Wearmouth (1961-62), Horden CW (1963), Enfield (1964), Penrith (1965), home-town Sunderland (1966-71) and Newark (1972) during his Durham career, Budgie's best back against the wall batting came in GC ties.

He top-scored against Sussex in 1964 with 28 out of 93, then made a similar battling 26 (out of 82) against Worcestershire in 1968. He had matured as a batsman by the 1970s, scoring 95 out of the winning 141/6 against Oxfordshire in 1972, winning the Man of the Match award.

While in 1965 he was the only specialist batsman to average over 30 and in 1967 scored over 400 at 43.10, backing Inglis' record 893, the forceful batsman changed Durham's fortunes in 1971 and 1972, linking with new signings Steve Greensword and Dave Halfyard. The county finished 3rd and 4th and Burridge hit 476 runs at 43.27 and 396 at 39.60.

He left Durham in 1972, with Russell Inglis following a year later. Burridge was in sixth place in the Durham runs aggregate list and Inglis top. Fortunately, Neil Riddell and Steve Atkinson debuted the year Burridge went to play for Lincolnshire, close to his club side Newark.

Work took him to Lincolnshire from 1973-74 and Hertfordshire from 1975-78, where he played for Watford CC for more than 20 years.

Middlesex CCC appointed him secretary in 1980. He later ran a sports centre in Watford.

100
GREATS

Bernard Lance Cairns
RHB & RFM, 1979-88

At the age of 29, Lance Cairns was a test player, but not a full-time cricketer. He found job-seeking tough after six months playing for New Zealand, so when Whitburn offered him a contract during the 1978 New Zealand tour of England, he fulfilled his ambition to become a full time pro. 'I always wanted to try, so I did it,' he said.

While wearing tight-fitting beige, Cairns went from the DSCL to helping New Zealand towards a 1979 World Cup semi-final loss to England. However, after just two overs in each DSCL match, the 'conkers' balls ('because they were like concrete') lost 'any semblance' of swing. 'A waste of time,' he said. But Paul Romaines had plans for Cairns and secretly set him up with Bishop Auckland for 1980. Although he was getting more than £100 a match in the GC, 'I was never one to try and blackmail a club. I had no idea what to ask a club moneywise and Paul Romaines suggested a figure, when I had a meeting with Bishop Auckland they said I suppose you want… and that was exactly what Paul had told me.'

'You'd think I was spy for Russia,' said Cairns, who returned for a 'magic year (120 wickets in 1980),' using the English Duke ball, which he said was 'made for me.'

'It was the most enjoyable cricket I've ever played, which reflects on the people I was playing with. It was always a laugh. Everybody was a joker and there was never a dull moment, with no bitchiness. Everybody got on in a team environment.'

Cairns said players from fashionable clubs filled the Durham side. 'If there was a choice made on a couple of players between Durham City and Philadelphia, Durham would definitely get the player in. South Shields always struggled to get players into the Durham side.'

Bernard Lance Cairns
Born: Picton, New Zealand, 10 October 1949
Also played for: Central Districts, Otago, Northern Districts, New Zealand

Batting

M	I	NO	Runs
35	39	2	803
Ave	100	50	
21.70	0	4	

Bowling

O	Md	R	W
902.1	276	2,362	135
Ave	5wI	10wM	Ct
17.49	9	2	28

Best Performances
88 *v.* Cumberland, 1979
7/61 *v.* Cumberland, 1980

Cairns worked at Whitburn emptying 44-gallon drums of sludge, and at Bishops, on captain and 'gentleman farmer' Graham Smith's (Durham 82-83) farm. 'We'd watch cricket and cut a bit of hay or corn, then bring the bales of hay home in the trailer. It was very enjoyable, but not hard work,' Cairns said.

'I loved the club makeup. If the professional at the club performed you put him on a pedestal. You'd do your bit for the club and they'd do your bit for you. Stories of pros sitting in at home in their flat – that's what they deserve because as a pro you're backing yourself to support yourself.

'I got into Durham team because I was playing test cricket. I wasn't 100mph and I couldn't bat for hours, I was completely self-taught, and played the game my way. I'd never been coached, but my ability to get some wickets because of movement in English conditions made my bowling pretty successful.'

Despite his simple approach, Cairns was good at finding opponents' weaknesses. In a club game for Bishops against Neil Riddell's Darlington, Cairns bowled off two paces, and zapped through the overs to ensure a finish. 'Riddell would have been ropeable – he was out-thought.'

Cairns bowled like a slowed down Mike Procter, using inswing to right handers and leg cutters to take his wickets. From having to be taught how to knot his tie for his test debut in 1973, by 1985 he'd played in every test country, and been on the winning side against all the top nations.

In 1988 Bishops signed Kapil Dev, but at the last minute he let them down. 'I'll play for you if you pay me what you were going to pay Kapil Dev,' Cairns said. 'And so I had a very, very good year (a League record 124 wickets) that year with them as far as money went.' He was eligible to play NWT for Durham too, and scored 54 in the loss to Somerset.

Riddell said: 'It was not just the way he played his cricket, nor was it because his brilliant three seasons with us made it easy to captain the side. The real impact he made on me was his positive attitude to life. He would never let a negative word pass his lips. Lance's greatest strength was he knew how to win, and that rubbed off on me and made me a better and more aware captain.'

Cairns' memories of Durham are overwhelmingly happy – after all 'they taught me how to drink pints'.

John Carr
RHB & RFM/OB, 1924-46

100 GREATS

Durham's Gary Sobers, tall, lean and unassuming, six-hit specialist Jack Carr started at Durham with a bang.

Already 30, Carr debuted against the South Africans scoring 28 at No.10 and taking 1/28. In the next 16 days he took 12/100 in his first

John Carr
Born: Leadgate, 29 May 1894
Died: Hartlepool, November 1967

Batting

M	I	NO	Runs
183	246	15	4,472
Ave	100	50	
19.35	4	14	

Bowling

O	Md	R	W
3,551.4	859	8,904	524
Ave	5wI	10wM	Ct
16.99	29	3	129

Best Performances
134 v. Yorkshire II, 1934
8/40 v. Yorkshire II, 1936

Championship game, a defeat to Northumberland, 10/58 in a win over Yorkshire II and 9/42 in another victory over Lancashire II at Barrow.

He'd rescued Durham's season and in 1926, with 42 wickets at under 14, alongside Albert Howell's 34 wickets, ever-present Carr helped take Durham to the title. Hon. Secretary William Bell said in his history of the county, 'It makes no difference to Carr who bowls, Carr hits. Cheered by the spectators for his sixes, sympathised with for his ducks, Carr is the most popular cricketer in Durham County today.'

He played a Durham record 183 matches, with Bertie Brooks' 121 (1906-29) next best, when Carr retired after playing five games in 1946, when he was 52. Only Neil Riddell and Steve Greensword beat it by Durham's move to first-class status in 1992.

Later switching to off spin, Carr was an accurate, intelligent bowler, who used artfulness and variation of pace rather than speed to exploit the uncovered pitches of the 1930s.

He was professional for Chester-le-Street when he made his county debut up to 1930, then played for Blackhall from 1931-42, Darlington RA from 1942-44 and Stockton in 1945, when he returned to Blackhall.

A hugely popular, key member of the Minor County Championship-winning sides of 1926 and 1930, Carr made an influential contribution with bat or ball or both. In 1926 his military medium off cutters brought 41 wickets and scored a century. In 1930 he scored two hundreds, but his bowling, particularly the quicker off cutter bowled with no change in action, brought him his biggest rewards.

Despite the Depression, Durham prospered, with a 12,000 Chester-le-Street Whitsun crowd paying a record £413 to see hometown hero Carr score 40 and take six wickets, Tom Dobson junior take eight and Len Weight score a century in an innings win in the derby match with Northumberland.

He took 34 wickets in 1925, and averaged around 30 wickets a season and 250-300 runs up to the Second World War. In 1934 he added 192 with Albert Elsdon in an innings win against Yorkshire II, which remained a seventh wicket record for over half a century. Carr showed his consistency with seven seven-wicket innings, behind only Alf Morris and William Whitwell. He stretched these analyses from 1924-41, with 12/100 (7/66 and 5/34) against Northumberland in 1924, 11/83 (7/23 and 4/60) against Staffordshire in 1937 and 10/58 (7/17, 3/41) against Yorkshire II in 1924.

He played a record 13 games in succession against touring teams. His dependable and remarkably consistent performances included 28 at No.10 and 1/21 against South Africa in the 1924 draw and 0 and 35 when promoted to No.8.

He took 1/41 (Charlie Macartney) against Australia in 1926, then hit 35 in ten minutes, including 17 off one memorable over from Clarrie Grimmett. In 1927 he took 3/56, including the wicket of Roger Blunt, against New Zealand, though Durham-born Blunt, whose father was a languages don at Durham University, dismissed Carr twice, for nought and one, as he rose still further up the batting order, to No.5.

Against the 1928 West Indians he scored four and 29 and took 3/20, then scored 35 and took 2/55 against New Zealand in 1931. His later performances declined save for an all-round effort that gave Durham a first international win in 1936. He took 2/39, then scored 45, adding 59 with his captain Tom Dobson junior, who made less than a quarter of the runs while the pair took Durham from 26/5 to 85/6 against India in 1936. In the second innings, Dobson moved Carr up the order as Durham chased 202. Carr whacked a quick 31 and Arnie Close and Albert Howell completed the 18 runs required for the win.

Carr once hit a ball at Feethams that dropped over the ball of the adjoining football ground – spectators used to watch purely to see Carr swing.

Even in 1946, Carr, the only survivor other than Close and Vijay Merchant from the 1936 Indian game, took 1/11 off 10 overs, removing future Durham guest Cottari (CS) Nayudu.

Arthur Austin told Jack Bannister that Carr, who always wore his cap at a jaunty angle, was an aggressive batsman: 'He was a marvellous cricketer and what a hitter. His favourite stroke was a six over cover point, and I remember being at the other end when he hit O'Reilly twice into the pavilion for six.'

In 1938 aged 44, Carr scored more than 300 runs and took 27 wickets at 21.37, but the impending war could not stop his cricket. In 1940 he took 6/35 as an amateur against Len Hutton and Hedley Verity's Catterick Garrison. Carr's 1946 testimonial yielded £271. Carr was a miner who became a licensed victualler who ran pubs in Hartlepool.

He died in 1967, the same year as fellow Durham stalwarts Ernest Proud and Brooks.

Robert Cole — 100 GREATS
RHB & WK, 1958-74

Standing up to the fastest of bowling, bubbly Bobby Cole's wicketkeeping is fondly remembered by Durham's following.

In all, even for a keeper, Cole held the Durham record for dismissals of 237, of catches (165), stumpings (72) and catches in an innings (six against Northumberland in 1968).

Cole was from a non-cricket area in the south west of the county, where he worked as an instructor in the construction industry.

A loyal Darlington cricketer throughout his career, Cole replaced Jackie Fox for Durham when Fox followed former Durham keeper Dick Spooner to Warwickshire. Although Fox won a Durham recall in 1964 after leaving Warwickshire in 1961, Cole regained his place afterwards.

The hard-to-shut-up Cole bridged the gap between the era of tourist matches and the Gillette Cup, being ever present in Durham's showpieces including the landmark win over Yorkshire in 1973. Batting No.11, he scored a single run in his nine major games.

He scored six runs in six innings in 1965, including just one in three games over four seasons, using his only real stroke, an onside waft known by the team as the 'Cole Shuttle'.

He broke most of Durham's wicketkeeping records. His career catches and stumping aggregates

Robert Cole			
Born: Ferryhill Station, 17 November 1938			
Batting			
M	I	NO	Runs
129	101	54	583
Bowling			
O	Ave	Ct	St
11	6.02	162	72

were far ahead of Johnny Common's 79 catches and Arthur Austin's 62 stumpings. His best seasons were 1966 and 1973 with 24 dismissals in each.

He made 319 NYSD League dismissals, including 168 catches and 151 stumpings.

Annual reports often noted Cole's high quality keeping. In 1973 he won the Player of the Year Award, for 'his high standard and consistent wicketkeeping.'

His captain Brian Lander said Cole had a great pair of hands. With his quicksilver takes and stumpings down leg, standing up to fast bowlers, and modest, unassuming, character, Cole, who captained Darlington in 1969 and 1976 was probably the best Durham keeper prior to 1992.

Paul David Collingwood — 100 GREATS
RHB & RM

A light-weight, ginger-haired, sociable all-rounder, Paul Collingwood found unexpected, but deserved success as an England one-day batsman, highlighted by his determined and resourceful batting in the 2003 World Cup.

As Durham captain Jon Lewis said; 'the perfect product of the modern game,' in that he can bat, field and bowl, each to match-winning effect in all forms of the game, showed the success of Durham's home-grown youth policy.

Collingwood's father, David, (who Collingwood could have followed into caravan making) used to

Paul David Collingwood
Born: Shotley Bridge, 26 May 1976
Also played for: England

Batting

M	I	NO	Runs
95	164	12	4,899
Ave	100	50	
32.23	8	28	

Bowling

O	Md	R	W
930.5	231	2,629	65
Ave	Ct		
40.04	96		

Best Performance
190 v. SL, 2002

coach Paul and his brother Peter in the prettiest corner of his hometown, the Shotley Bridge CC nets. His mother made the teas for the Tyneside Senior League team.

Picked as a middle-order batsman and medium pace outswing bowler, 'Colly' made his one-day debut in 1995 and his first-class debut in 1996.

He bowled former England allrounder David Capel with his first ball, and scored 91 and 16 against Northants. Though he made only one more first-class fifty and took two more wickets that season, it was a hugely encouraging start for fans of a county craving home-grown all-round talent.

But with expectations high, Collingwood took several years to make the grade. In 1997, coach Norman Gifford used Collingwood as an opener before a finger injury ended his season in July. In 1998, he began against Warwickshire with a maiden century, guided by captain David Boon to a county sixth wicket record of 193. Collingwood said Boon helped his sense of self-belief grow. The pair helped regain Durham pride against Warwickshire, after Brian Lara's 501* in 1994. Collingwood then showed his growing maturity with 97* to see Durham to a decisive lead against Nottinghamshire at Trent Bridge in May, but he struggled to score at home on the suspect Riverside pitch.

Durham members voted him Player of the Year in 2000, when he showed his one-day potential with 607 runs, second only for Durham to Dean Jones' 656 in 1992. He made 1,000 first-class runs for the first time in 2001, but played little for Durham in 2002 and 2003 due to injury and international calls.

In 2001 he began with 130, 22, 68, 95 and 153 off 261 balls with 20x4 and 1x6 against Mel Betts and co. at Edgbaston. His one-day form was equally

impressive winning him selection for the NatWest series against Pakistan and Australia. His ODI career began badly, but he later won revenge on the winter tour of Zimbabwe. Collingwood scored 77 and a swashbuckling 56* off 46 balls which carried England to victory and a 5-0 whitewash in the final game at Bulawayo. Carrying on to India, his match-winning unbeaten 71 against India at Cuttack won him the Man of the Match award. He was again Man of the Match against New Zealand in Napier after his outswingers bowled England to victory taking 4-38 in the third ODI. 'I've been working hard on my bowling with the coach and hopefully I will get another yard. I am a genuine swinger of the ball and there are still flaws in my action,' he said.

Life and soul of the party and a bit of a jack the lad, Collingwood played in every match of the 2002 NatWest triangular series, including becoming the first Durham player to play an ODI at Riverside against India on 4 July 2002. Although a neck injury ruled him out of the ICC Champions Trophy, he became Durham's most successful home-grown international with innings like his 66*, which set up England's sole win against a major cricket nation, Pakistan, in the 2003 World Cup.

'The World Cup was a fantastic education with a lot of situations which will make me stronger for the future,' he said.

One aspect of Collingwood's game is sometimes forgotten – he was the first Durham fielder to reach 100 catches (in all matches). However, his committed fielding backfired when he dislocated a shoulder diving to stop an Andy Flintoff drive in a pre-season friendly at Old Trafford in April 2003, leaving him sidelined for a 'dream come true' first test appearance, on 5 June against Zimbabwe at the Riverside. However, he returned at the end of 2003, won a somewhat unlikely England contract (ahead of Harmison) and came close to making a test debut on the tour of Bangladesh, where his ability to work the ball mid-innings again won him a regular ODI place, blending with Flintoff as graft/bash batting partners.

Collingwood then batted doggedly in two tests against Sri Lanka in late 2003 and toured West Indies early the next year.

Geoffrey Cook

RHB & SLA, 1991

Geoffrey Cook
Born: Middlesbrough, 9 October 1951
Also played for: Northamptonshire, Eastern Province, England

Batting

M	I	NO	Runs
24	24	9	782
Ave	100	50	Ct
52.13	1	3	25

One Day (1992)

M	Runs	HS	Ave	Ct
3	79	49	26.33	1

Best Performance
101 v. Surrey, 1991

The former secretary and chairman of the Cricketer's Association returned to his native North-East in 1991 as Durham's Director of Cricket to prepare for the club's maiden season as a first-class county.

With David Graveney, Cook chose the Durham squad and coached the team. The role of cricket director and coach was probably too much for one man and meant Cook had to give up playing in 1992, although he turned out three times in emergencies.

Although officially retired from first-team cricket, Graveney asked Cook to play in a Sunday League game against Leicestershire, with Dean Jones and Phil Bainbridge injured. Cook's experience brought him the top score of 49 before John Glendenen ran him out. Afterwards, Cook chose to let young players have a chance.

But it was as an intense thinker about the game that Cook shaped Durham's early years. He had headed to Northants from the North-East in the early 1970s, where he joined Ollie Milburn, Peter Willey, George Sharp, Alan Hodgson and Alan Tait. He partnered Wayne Larkins at the top of the order, working the ball around whilst Larkins hit the big shots.

After seven tests and a best season of 1,759 runs at 43.97 in 1981 (when he was county captain), England banned him after the 1982 rebel tour to South Africa.

Cook enjoyed talking about the game and had a good memory for statistics and what players had achieved. He thought hard about the past and what players could bring to the future of Durham.

Later, as the guide to young players at the club, Cook said he was proud he had been first to welcome and watch develop most of Durham's cricketers, including increasing numbers born within the county. He said: 'One of the core aims of Durham is to now contribute significantly to English cricket.' In this area, Durham (and Cook), thanks to giving locals Brown, Harmison and Collingwood sustained opportunity, has succeeded.

John Cook
Born: Preston, date unknown
Died: Preston, date unknown

Batting

M	I	NO	Runs
35	48	16	552
Ave	100	50	
17.25	1	1	

Bowling

O	Md	R	W
1,044.3	390	1,912	103
Ave	5wI	10wM	Ct
18.56	4	1	24

Best Performances
106* v. New Zealand, 1927
8/42 v. Lancashire II, 1926

Jack Cook was a professional bowler, but only a useful lower order batsman. Yet his biggest contribution for Durham came from No.10 in the order, with Durham 58/8, 315 behind the touring New Zealanders. He had taken 4/96, including the wicket of future Gloucestershire player Cec Dacre. With only one-match wonder South Shields' Joe Legg (he scored a pair and didn't bowl) to come, Cook set about Herb McGirr, Matt Henderson, Roger Blunt, Bill Cunningham and three more tried by Dacre, who was standing in for New Zealand captain/manager Tom Lowry. Cook outscored his captain Bertie Brooks and made Durham's first century against an official touring team, before Blunt caught Brooks 20 short of the follow-on to end Durham's record ninth wicket stand of 195. Legg went a run later. Cook scored 7* in the follow-on and bowled one over as Charlie Oliver and Bill Bernau scored the five runs needed to win. His day of glory was over.

From a cricket family, Cook's brothers Bill and Lol played for Lancashire as medium fast bowlers in the early part of the twentieth century. His father, Bill senior, was groundsman at Preston CC for over thirty years. He was one of five brothers and learnt the game in Preston, before becoming a pro at Bollington in Cheshire aged seventeen. The story is complicated by the likelihood that Cook was registered at birth as John Whalley, Whalley being Lol's middle name. His brothers' names were not registered at birth, probably due to the expense.

Cook played in and for Cheshire then moved to West Hartlepool as pro in 1925. In 1926 he took 42 wickets at under 14 for Durham (40 in Minor Counties matches), and with Albert Howell, his fellow debutant taking 34; Durham had enough firepower to take the Championship.

That season, against Northumberland, he took 5/90 helping set up a win, and his 8/42 against Lancashire II earnt a first innings lead of 46. Durham set Lancashire 168, and then Cook and Jack Carr reduced them to 19/4. Cook ended the win with his best match figures -11/68.

The following year, Leveson Gower's XI played at Ashbrooke, holding out at 102/7 as Cook took a full part in tackling Jack Hobbs, Andy Sandham, Frank Woolley, Stan Worthington, Andy Ducat, and Jack MacBryan – the finest batting line-up seen in the county.

An opening bowler of splendid control, Cook disappointed in 1927 with 19 wickets in 320.2 overs, but his century was part of 347 runs overall at 43.37. Otherwise he scored 205 runs over three seasons in 34 innings. After the New Zealand century he won promotion to No.7 and scored 49 against Yorkshire II. In 1928, against Yorkshire firsts, Cook's batting paid off even more effectively, even though he made just one not out. Yorkshire needed to bat again to score that run, but as Jack Carr was out at 6.23pm there wasn't enough time left for Yorkshire to win.

Durham was third in the Championship, but the bowling declined with Howell and Cook's returns diminished. Cook left after 1929 and was later a professional/coach in Lancashire.

An affluent glassmaker, typical Victorian cricket captain Tom Coulson played cricket for recreation.

'Played purely for the love of the game, win or lose was of no consequence to him, play the game and hang the points was his motto,' said William Bell in his history of the club. Despite this carefree attitude to winning, Durham won the Championship in Coulson's first year as a player, although he scored only 81 runs in seven innings.

Thomas Coulson
Born: South Shields, 1867
Died: South Shields, 13 February 1919

Batting

M	I	NO	Runs	Ct
87	143	11	1,855	25

Best Performance
86 v. Northumberland, 1906

Coulson lived and died in a house overlooking the South Shields cricket club and was steeped in the history of Shields throughout his life.

When Coulson succeeded Edgar Elliot as Durham captain in 1907 his strategy appeared to be simple. He bowled Alf Morris hard and hoped the batsmen could score enough runs without Elliot to make a good game of it. Durham's best finish under Coulson was sixth, in his final year of captaincy, 1911.

As a batsman Coulson's record is modest. He was hit on the head by a rising ball at Jesmond in 1908 and was never the same player again.

Durham's committee awarded Coulson a silver rose bowl in 1912 for his services as player/captain. In 1913, Coulson was part of an unpleasant incident at Philadelphia's Bunker Hill ground, when he refused to let South Shields bat again after Durham wicketkeeper 'Kellet' Kirtley incited a riot as a protest against unfair umpiring decisions. The clash was probably more indicative of the class difference between the clubs, embodied by rough miner Kirtley and rich factory owner Coulson.

Coulson served on the Durham committee until his death, in the shadow of the South Shields club he ran. His son Forster was also a Durham player and administrator.

Alexander Coxon
RHB & RFM, 1951-54

Durham secured the services of a fast bowler who had been a test player three seasons earlier in 1951, a signing that would make even today's first-class side envious.

But Alec Coxon had a reputation that meant no one else wanted him. For someone as stubborn and cantankerous as Coxon's former Yorkshire teammate Brian Close to say 'he was as harsh and grating of manner as he was of speech, as hard and uncompromising a competitor in conversation as he was a bowler,' suggests Coxon's personality contained most of the worst of Yorkshiremen's archetypal characteristics. He seldom gave autographs, lest they might be sold, and when asked for an interview prior to the 2001 Ashes, refused should he be exploited. Taking everything to its extreme, Coxon now prints his signature on bills to render it worthless. The Fred Trueman prototype ('Freddie picked up a few tips from Alec,' said Malcolm Scott)

Alexander Coxon
Born: Huddersfield, 18 January 1916
Also played for: Yorkshire, England

Batting

M	I	NO	Runs
29	40	4	1,047
Ave	**100**	**50**	
29.08	2	7	

Bowling

O	Md	R	W
913.4	279	1,885	127
Ave	**5wI**	**10wM**	
14.84	9	2	

Best Performances
122* v. Yorkshire II, 1952
9/28 v. Staffordshire, 1952

argued violently with Denis Compton in the 1948 Lord's Test dressing room, and was never to play for England again. John Arlott reported on an England player saying 'his face didn't fit.' For half a century Coxon claimed he had Don Bradman lbw; a prime example of the chip on his shoulder. Mike Tate said Coxon described how he had angrily called Bradman 'a lucky bugger', something that 'sealed his fate' at the top.

At Durham, Coxon formed a hostile duo when paired with fellow Yorkshire discard Ron Aspinall. As Sunderland professional, bowling fast off a long run, with immaculate length, Coxon menaced both opposition batsmen and his own slips when they dropped catches.

He scored 50 showing his correct technique and upright stance at No.3 against India in 1952, and then took 5/40 off 49.5 overs (26 maidens) in the winning draw. Aspinall took 6/84 in India's first innings, after which Durham led by 146 runs.

'Coxon was a personality; on entering the ground one sensed immediately here was a man in charge of proceedings. Never did he relax for one moment and to him the opponents were the enemy,' wrote D.G. Greig in Sunderland CC's history, *To Ashbrooke and Beyond.*

He was the league's highest paid pro, and repaid Sunderland by only missing one match in eight seasons (DSCL 3,764 runs at 34.2, 753 wickets at 8.3), except to appear on county duty. Coxon was also a very good coach in the nets and winter school, helping Durham's Peter Birtwisle and Scott amongst others.

The epitome of the inflexible, irascible Tyke, Coxon rarely erred at Durham after upsetting the Yorkshire administration so much they let him go after taking 131 wickets at 18 in 1950. However, Cocko's temper finally snapped in 1954 when Durham met Lancashire II on a wet Old Trafford pitch. Lancashire's Roy Collins hit a big hundred, annoying Coxon. After a shower the players went back on and found the pitch laughably soft. Coxon asked for sawdust, which a boy brought on. Coxon said 'put the fucker there,' pointing to a good length on the wicket. The boy did as he was told and the players had to leave the field for 20 minutes whilst it was cleared. Captain Bill Proud tore into Coxon, who never played for the county again. Scott thought Coxon was just being 'a

mischievous bugger; sometimes he and Aspinall got a bit bored'.

It had happened before. Tony Woodhouse describes Coxon's departure from Yorkshire thus: 'His fiery temperament had got the better of him.' Coxon was coaching in South Africa in the winter of 1950/51. Weeks later he was in Sunderland, where he lived into old age. He took 100 wickets for Sunderland each season from 1952-54, then played for South Shields from 1958-64, then Wearmouth, taking 71 wickets in 1966 aged 50.

Off the pitch Coxon was a 'hugely sociable man with a lively, mischievous sense of humour and fun and an absorbing raconteur,' said Clive Crickmer in his *History of South Shields Cricket.* Aged seventy-six in 1992, Coxon took a three-year appointment as junior coach at South Shields and was still a vocal spectator at Wood Terrace a decade later.

A call to Coxon in 2003 brought this response: 'I'm not interested. Sorry. Bye.' Perhaps (with 'sorry') signs of mellowing? Maybe in 10 years Coxon will be ready to tell his story.

The former Bradford City centre forward won his cap for Yorkshire when captain Brian Sellars gave Coxon his Yorkshire cap by taking off his own cap and putting it on his craggy opening bowler's head. 'It fits okay. You keep it, you've earned it,' said Sellars, recognising a fellow Yorkshire martyr.

George Crawford

RHB, 1953-66

A commercial artist for ICI all his working life, George Crawford had one season of artistry on the pitch for Durham, when he won the 1961 Wilfred Rhodes Trophy for topping the Minor Counties averages.

It was the tall, correct Billingham Synthonia right hander's year, as he scored two centuries, including 102 against Lancashire II, when he and Alan Burridge added 223 for the fourth wicket, 27 short of Tommie Bradford and Cecil Brooks' 1910 record.

Crawford was a product of Hartlepool Technical School and made his Durham debut aged eighteen after catching the selectors eye following catching the bus from Norton with Gus Williamson to practice at Durham School.

It took until 1961 for his game to mature, though he never quite fulfilled his potential. Dark and swarthy, Crawford was a talented close-to-the-wicket fielder and an all rounder at club level, though his bowling was not used as much as it might have been for Durham. As a batsman he could tailor his game to suit the needs of the side, scoring freely or blocking as necessary.

Of 1961, Crawford said: 'I just couldn't not get runs. I had an average of 80-odd. Geoff Boycott was lower down. People classed me as a stroke player who scored all round the wicket. That year the ball seemed very big and the bowlers seemed to bowl straight at me. Against Lancashire they had a leg

George Crawford			
Born: Haverton Hill, 10 January 1935			
Batting			
M	I	NO	Runs
57	86	9	1,733
Ave	100	50	Ct
22.50	2	4	38
Best Performance			
149* v. Cumberland, 1961			

spinner on (Tommy Greenhough) who got Bell and Keeler out. Burridge came in. I'd been hitting it in the middle and told him he isn't turning it, just play straight and Alan got 120. I wished I'd had a lot more seasons like that.'

Crawford now lives at Wingate near Peterlee. At 52 he retired from ICI to the golf course and to coach Durham County golf juniors. He still plays golf with former Durham players including Billy Wake, Alan Campbell, John Camburn and Ken Longstaff.

He said: 'It was a great pleasure being involved at Durham, just playing with a lot of people as enthusiastic as me.'

His answer phone message says: 'As usual we're all out at present, but if you have any messages for the incoming batsmen please feel free to leave them.'

Hugh Lloyd Dales

LHB & SLA, 1911-14

One of the earliest Durham-bred cricketers to play full-time professional county cricket, Hughie (or Horace at Middlesex) Dales toured the West Indies in 1925/26 and had a long and productive career with Middlesex. He became one of the list of internationals lost to Durham, including Parkin, Spooner and Milburn.

He learnt his cricket with Durham, scoring almost 1,000 runs in 29 innings before the First World War. He grew sounder each year, making his first century, 118 against Cambridge in 1913, when he averaged 51.60 and 127 in his last game for the county, against Cheshire in 1914.

Dales' father Tom was wicketkeeper for Medomsley and was once picked for Durham, but never played, possibly due to work commitments.

The attractive and prolific former Consett club player played some startling innings for Middlesex,

Hugh Lloyd Dales			
Born: Medomsley, 18 May 1888			
Died: Whitley Bay, 4 May 1964			
Also played for: Middlesex			
Batting			
M	I	NO	Runs
22	32	3	943
Ave	100	50	
32.51	2	5	
Bowling			
O	Md	R	W
10	0	45	0
Ave	Ct		
n/a	8		
Best Performance			
127 v. Cheshire, 1914			

including 103, adding 175 with Harry Lee in Middlesex's 642/3 against Hants at Southampton in 1922. Patsy Hendren (177*) and J.W. (Jack) Hearne (232) then put on a world record 375 for the third wicket.

In 1923 he scored 1,138 runs at 29.17 and in 1924 hit three centuries for Middlesex.

Dales' career highlight was the 1925/26 MCC tour to the West Indies. He won selection as a like-able amateur, however, of the 13 games played under Frederick Gough-Calthorpe, Dales played just six, scoring 149 runs with a best of 50 against Trinidad in Port of Spain, when Walter Hammond made half-centuries in both innings.

Hammond was thought to have caught syphilis on the tour, which affected him for the rest of his life. The rest of the team was of strong county stan-dard and included Lionel Lord Tennyson and Tiger Smith. The team lost by an innings and 73 to Barbados, with George Challenor who played at Feethams in 1923 and Ashbrooke in 1928 against Durham, scoring 124.

Dales worked as a schoolmaster, becoming head-master of Waterhouses School.

100 GREATS

Thomas Kell Dobson
LHB & OB, 1922-36

Thomas Kell Dobson
Born: South Shields, 27 January 1901
Died: Sunderland, 3 October 1940

Batting

M	I	NO	Runs
100	148	24	3,040
Ave	100	50	
24.51	5	15	

Bowling

O	Md	R	W
1,796.3	550	3,775	226
Ave	5wI	10wM	Ct
16.70	8	2	47

Best Performances
114* v. Yorkshire II, 1932
7/25 v. Staffordshire, 1931

The youngest former captain at death, at 39, all-rounder Tom Dobson played a century of matches for Durham from 1922-36, the last of six Dobsons to represent the county. His father and three uncles played prior to the First World War and his younger brother William from 1919-25. Only Jack Carr and C.L. Adamson matched Dobson's number of appearances for Durham before the Second World War.

He was a middle-order batsman whose father, Thomas Kell Dobson senior played 21 times for Durham between 1886-96, top scoring with 117* against Yorkshire at Darlington in 1892. Yorkshire held on to draw, but Dobson's stands of 103 with Harry Wilson and 81 with William Whitwell had given Yorkshire a scare.

T.K. senior was son of the head gardener on Sir Hedworth Williamson's estate, Whitburn Hall near Sunderland. The assistant accountant for the North Eastern Railway in Newcastle committed suicide on 23 December 1921 by stepping from the platform at Carlisle station into the path of a train. One of his two sons looked on, helpless. The committee said he lived for cricket in its tribute.

Thomas junior, then aged twenty, was just begin-ning his career with Durham. In his 15 years there, which included five as captain, Thomas junior did his father's name proud.

He hit five centuries for the county, including 105 against the West Indies at Ashbrooke in 1928 after coming in at 28/4. Dobson became the only amateur to take 200 wickets and score 3,000 runs for Durham. He also played for Leveson-Gower's XI at Scarborough and the Minor Counties. Similar to his father in style, Dobson became Durham's best all rounder yet before illness ended his career.

He had been working in Martin's Bank until three days before his death, which followed three years of poor health. He was buried in the same grave as his father at Whitburn. His mother outlived him.

Alexander Graham Doggart

RHB & RM, 1919-24

One of the most remarkable of Durham cricketers, Graham Doggart won fame as a cricketer, footballer, sports administrator and businessman.

He was a first-class cricketer at Cambridge University and Middlesex and scored two centuries in seven games for Durham.

Heading a family of cricketers, Doggart's son Hubert, played for Sussex and England against the West Indies in 1950, and was later President of the MCC. Another of Doggart's sons, Arthur, who killed himself in 1965, also played for Sussex and wrote for *The Cricketer*. Graham's brother James, a London eye specialist, played for Cambridge University in 1919 and Durham from 1919-22. The youngest brother, Norman, was Darlington captain (he also played for Darlington FC) from 1940-47 and played for Durham from 1933-40. Graham's grandson Simon won cricket blues at Cambridge from 1980-83. The Doggart family was one of Durham's great sporting dynasties, and rank with the Roseberry, Weston, and Whitwell families for their contribution to sport in the county.

Graham Doggart played inside left for Corinthians and England at football against Belgium in 1924 and won Cambridge University Blues at cricket (1921-22), rugby, fives, rackets, squash and football.

Rarely available, for business reasons, Doggart showed his batting skill with 37 and 37* against the 1921 Australians, who included Ted McDonald, Warwick Armstrong and Arthur Mailey, and his bowling prowess with 3/21 off 19.1 overs against the

Alexander Graham Doggart			
Born: Bishop Auckland, 2 June 1897			
Died: London, 7 June 1963			
Also played for: Cambridge University, Minor Counties, Middlesex			

Batting			
M	I	NO	Runs
7	11	1	364
Ave	100	50	
36.40	2	0	

Bowling			
O	Md	R	W
116.1	21	392	17
Ave	5wl	10wM	Ct
23.05	0	0	10

Best Performance
129 v. Northumberland, 1922

1924 South Africans. He was a better player than his style suggested, 'a batsman who is not easily put off his game,' wrote Digby Jephson in *The Cricketer*.

As 1928 President of the British Baptist Union, he advocated temperance from the pulpit and was a generous, charitable businessman. He worked as an accountant and director of the 'fair deal' Quaker family firm Doggart Stores (founded by his father in 1895), a 14-shop chain in the North-East.

Doggart died whilst chairing the 1963 Football Association AGM.

Edgar William Elliot

RHB & RMF, 1897-1907

'The most brilliant batsman who ever played for Durham,' wrote William Bell in his history of Durham CCC's first fifty years.

'There are no words of praise other than the old ones. He was the most felicitous of sportsmen; the idol of Durham cricket fields; as handsome in skill and individual in style as any great batsman moving in more exalted circles. He was idolatrously admired for the beauty and power of his batting and drew record crowds wherever he went,' wrote D.G. Greig in the *History of Sunderland Cricket and Rugby Football Club*.

Born where the Stadium of Light now stands and educated at Wellington College, where he made the first XI in 1895 and 1896, Durham's greatest batsman pre-First World War, Edgar 'Tegger'

Elliot's cricket career was interrupted by service in salt mines and the Boer War.

Between 1897 and 1907 he scored 5,375 runs for the county, with two double centuries, still the most in 2004. He excelled against Surrey II, scoring 94 and 156* at the Oval in 1898, and 21 and 126 at the same ground the following year. In the two home games against the same team he hit 71, 86 and 13, giving a total of 567 at 94.5.

In 1898, he also scored 139 against Cambridge and made further centuries in 1903, 1904, 1906 and 1907, including a Durham record 217* (out of 338-3) against Lancashire II at Wearmouth in 1906.

In 1902, he served in South Africa with Fincastle's Horse. In 1903, Elliot, in his first year of four as captain, and his brother, Harry, playing for

Edgar William Elliot			
Born: Sunderland, 9 July 1878			
Died: Vancouver, Canada, 23 March 1931			

Batting

M	I	NO	Runs
94	162	16	5,384
Ave	100	50	
36.87	9	30	

Bowling

O	Md	R	W
133.3	36	330	15
Ave	Ct		
22.00	36		

Best Performance

217* v. Lancashire II, 1906

Durham for the first time since 1899, added 240 for the second wicket against Northumberland. Edgar made 204, the first double century for the county. Only John Glendenen's 200* against Victoria in 1991 equalled the feat in Durham's pre-first-class days.

In 1905 Elliot scored 332 in 225 minutes for the Borderers *v.* Newcastle Garrison at Jesmond. When Sunderland met Norton, strengthened by England's Bernard Bosanquet, Charlie Townsend and Reggie Spooner, Elliot made 96*, one of many great innings in the 6,263 runs he scored for Sunderland from 1896-1907.

Elliot followed brother Harry to Chile in 1907 after scoring 71 and 121 in his last game for the county, against Northumberland. 'The loss of E.W. Elliot's sparkling batting, together with some bad weather, had an effect on the gates,' lamented

Hon. Secretary William Bell. At the end of 1907 the county was £316 16s 5d in credit, which decreased to £50 17s 9d when the war started. Crowd numbers dropped when Elliot did not play – he was largely responsible for the great increase in cricket popularity in Durham after 1900.

He won four caps for England at rugby union as a winger from 1901-04, scoring two tries. Elliot played 29 times for Durham County, including twice in County Championship finals, scoring 20 tries. He also played four times for the Barbarians.

Once, against Lancashire II in the 1930s, a Durham player plodded to 90* by tea. A county official said the batsman's effort was approaching Elliot's, but an elderly Ashbrooke member said: 'If Elliot's body was now being wheeled in its coffin across the Town Moor, every bugger in the ground would leave at once and go down to see it.'

Elliot died in 1931 after working in Chile, Nairobi, the USA and for many years as a manager of salt mines in Canada.

100

GREATS

Stanley Ellis

LHB & RM/OB, 1929-37

In seven seasons with Lancashire (1892-98) Stan Ellis' father Jeremy played just six games, but still took 21 wickets at 11.42, including one analysis of 8/21. This was when he wasn't keeping wicket, where he made eight catches and three stumpings. His older son Walker, born in the family home at Summerseat, was in his last season of four as an opening batsman when Stan, a year younger at 27, played the first of his eight games for Lancashire in 1923.

None of the Ellis' made it at Lancashire, but Stan found the county success his father and brother

sought when he moved to Durham in 1929, following Frank Harry's career path. A diminutive medium pace off-break bowler, Ellis helped Durham to a championship at the same time Lancashire was in the middle of its greatest title-winning run.

Durham secretary Jack Iley, who rarely said anything good about anybody, rated Ellis highly, and there was little higher praise than that for a Durham player.

At Lancashire the small and wiry Ellis bowled with Cecil Parkin, and some of Parkin's hard bitten professionalism rubbed off on the Eppleton, Durham City and Horden CW professional.

Loud appealer Ellis linked with another former county bowler, Albert Howell, taking 45 wickets to Howell's 46 in 1929, but still looked on in envy as the county that did not re-engage him in 1925 took four Championships from 1926-30.

In 1930, alongside Howell and Ernie Hutchinson, Ellis bowled Durham to five consecutive wins to start 1930, against Northumberland, Lancashire, Yorkshire, Staffordshire and Northumberland. He took 8/71 in the match against Surrey II to clinch Durham's second title in five years, giving the county's following some cheer in the midst of the Depression.

In 1931, he shared 19 wickets with Tom Dobson against Barnes' Staffordshire and, satisfyingly for him and Durham, routed Lancashire II with 12/43 including a hat trick in 44 overs at South Shields. He took 38 wickets at 10.11 that year; in 1933 injury and illness held him back – he returned in 1934 with over 30 wickets. In high profile tourist matches he flourished with 3/40 in 1929 3/49 in 1935 against South Africa and 4/73, the most wickets by a Durham bowler, in the inaugural 1936 win over India. He later returned to the Lancashire leagues.

Stanley Ellis			
Born: Summerseat, 12 February 1896			
Died: Wilpshire, 14 February 1987			
Batting			
M	I	NO	Runs
68	78	31	432
Ave			
9.19			
Bowling			
O	Md	R	W
2,134	749	3,997	294
Ave	5wI	10wM	Ct
13.59	20	5	22
Best Performance			
7/19 v. Yorkshire II, 1930			

Henry Cecil Ferens CBE

RHB & WK, 1923-31

A private man who never married, Cecil Ferens served Durham county and city cricket as a player and administrator for over half a century.

Educated at Durham School, the short and plump Ferens brought Jack Iley to Durham County as secretary, thus providing Durham's gruff public face for forty years after the Second World War. Iley, a cantankerous, diffident, abrupt and sometimes unpopular man outside the county, shaped Durham post-war by having a say (along with captain Brian Lander) in the number of Durham City players who won late call-ups to the county side. He formed the image of the county team in the days when the secretary virtually ran the club. Ferens had a more honorary role as a county committeeman, Hon. Treasurer (1957-63) and Chairman (1964-75). He was also a Mayor of Durham City and solicitor for the Durham diocesan registry, which had offices in the heart of Durham city. Iley was his secretary there and in turn became his secretary at Durham CCC.

From a wealthy mill-owning family, Ferens captained the county from 1929-31, leading it to the 1930 title. He won the toss 10 times out of 11 at the opening of the 1925 season and batted each time. A broken finger ended his tenure in 1931,

Henry Cecil Ferens CBE			
Born: Durham City, 1899			
Died: Durham City, 1975			
Batting			
M	I	NO	Runs
61	90	11	2,034
Ave	100	50	Ct	St
25.74	1	8	62	12
Best Performance			
113* v. Leicestershire, 1925			

when Tom Dobson led in all but two games.

As a batsman Ferens favoured the onside, probably because of his heavy build, but played solid, correct cricket and won recognition for his talent as a wicketkeeper/batsman with selection for Minor Counties North. In 1927 he played at Ashbrooke for Durham against HDG Leveson-Gower's XI, which included Jack Hobbs, Frank Woolley, Andy Sandham, Herbert Strudwick and Andy Ducat. Ferens saw it as a 'privilege' to serve Durham City as a player from 1919-47, captain from 1923-46, as chairman for 35 years and president from 1958-75.

Andrew Robert Fothergill
RHB & WK, 1982-91

Andrew Robert Fothergill				
Born: Newcastle upon Tyne, 10 February 1962				
Batting				
M	I	NO	Runs	
75	61	24	394	
Ave	100	50	Ct	St
10.64	0	1	97	43
First Class (1992/93)				
M	I	NO	Runs	
12	17	1	127	
Ave	100	50	Ct	St
7.93	0	0	16	3

One of the few players from Durham's Minor County days to make the cut for its 1992 first-class bow, Andy Fothergill's good humour and naïveté cheered teammates and fans through the 1990s.

From the early 1980s, the Feethams product appeared to spectators set to replace the ageing Richard Mercer as county wicketkeeper. In 1984 the committee said Fothergill had 'done remarkably well when called upon to deputise for the injured Mercer, and the experience should prove most beneficial for the future.'

A former centre forward with Crook Town, he played his part with two catches in the 1985 NWT win over Derbyshire and by 1987 he was regular keeper, taking 14 catches and eight stumpings in the season.

At club level, the powerful fast scoring batsman made 1,882 runs and 218 dismissals for Darlington. At Minor County level, his batting rarely featured, with a single half century, and he showed his rawness when standing in the wrong position to the clutch of new bowlers in 1992. His batting reflected his personality, daft and eccentric; he used to hit the ball where it shouldn't go. He batted in the style of Alan Knott, though without the same success.

Outgoing, confident and helped by Knott, Fothergill improved throughout 1992, working mainly on his concentration and batting.

He played mainly Sunday League games, with Chris Scott the first-class keeper. In the opening Sunday game he put on 58 in 7.4 overs with Glendenen, showing the value of retaining local talent. Later, Fothergill caught four and stumped one Warwickshire batsmen without conceding a bye at Edgbaston.

Workwise, Fothergill was a bit of a 'Delboy', selling supermarket shelves, then working in the marketing department at Durham CCC before becoming a sports clothing representative; a job that suited his extrovert personality and love of sport.

Harry Gibbon
RHB & RM, 1925-38

Like Maurice Nichol, a product of the post First World War coaching scheme, Harry Gibbon served Durham and several northern clubs for fifteen years prior to the Second World War.

An amateur for Eppleton, New Seaham Park, then a professional for Sunderland, Eppleton and Bacup, Gibbon played in a Championship-winning team in just his second season with Durham.

Of mining stock, as one would expect from a boy from Hetton-le-Hole, Gibbon was an excellent league cricketer with a wide range of strokes, who was especially strong on the onside. Stocky and of average height, Gibbon hit his first century for Durham in 1928 – against Yorkshire's Emmott Robinson, George Macaulay and Wilfred Rhodes. Durham drew, after setting Yorkshire one run to win at 6.23pm, too late for a result.

Macaulay featured in a humorous Durham story. A young Durham University Cricket Club (DUCC) cap-wearing batsman tentatively walked to the wicket where Macaulay, a hard-bitten Tyke, was bowling. The batsman prodded and missed at Macaulay's probing deliveries until the last ball of the over beat him. As he bashfully left the pitch Macaulay pointed to the batsman's cap and said, 'I know thou scored a duck, but there's nay need t'shout about it.'

Gibbon's greatest triumph was yet to come. In the challenge match against Surrey II in 1930 Gibbon put on 157 with C.L. Adamson, scoring 97, then made 68 in the second innings to give Durham a win by 301 runs and a second title in five years.

Gibbon's bowling came on in later years, while his batting stayed consistent, a typical result being 1932's 380 runs at 23.75. He saved his best later performances for Denbighshire, scoring a century in 1934 and taking 7/16 in 1935. Gibbon retired in 1938.

He later became a warehouseman after spending much of his working life as a professional cricketer.

Harry Gibbon
Born: Hetton-le-Hole, c.1905
Died: Barrow, 1970s

Batting

M	I	NO	Runs
97	150	8	3,334
Ave	100	50	
23.47	2	19	

Bowling

O	Md	R	W
445.1	102	1,096	57
Ave	5wI	10wM	Ct
19.22	2	0	26

Best Performances
108 v. Yorkshire II, 1928
108 v. Denbighshire, 1934
7/16 v. Denbighshire, 1935

John David Glendenen

RHB & RM, 1988-91

100 GREATS

John David Glendenen
Born: Middlesbrough, 20 June 1955
Also played for: Yorkshire II, Cumberland

M	I	NO	Runs
49	78	9	2,472
Ave	100	50	Ct
35.82	5	10	32

First Class (1992/93)

M	I	NO	Runs
21	34	2	648
Ave	100	50	Ct
20.25	1	3	6

Best Performances
200* v. Victoria, 1991
117 v. OU, 1992 (First Class)

John Glendenen was an otherwise unfulfilled batsman with two claims to fame. He scored Durham's first double century for 85 years against Victoria in 1991, and then made the county's first first-class century. It was to be his last.

The former Portakabin salesman had trials with Gloucestershire and played for Yorkshire II, before batting successfully for Durham from 1988. However, senior professionals Phil Bainbridge and Geoff Cook felt Glendenen lacked the concentration to make a big innings. Nevertheless, the 200 showed he could do it and Cook gave Glendenen two enjoyable years on the staff.

In his first Benson and Hedges match he dropped two catches as Glamorgan won by four wickets, to earn the scorn of captain Graveney. In 1992, Graveney noticed Glendenen began playing round his front leg, resulting in lbw decisions. Nevertheless, Glendenen batted well in adversity, making a Championship best 64 against Somerset after scratching an eye in practice. However, 'Glendo' was too keen on enjoying the professional cricketer's lifestyle, fecklessly taking every opportunity to socialise. While old hands Ian Botham and Wayne Larkins could handle late nights, Glendenen's play suffered. He lost his fluency, and his place, although the chipper opener started the innings well on Sundays, finishing behind Jones

only in 1992, with 424 runs at 38.54 scoring 89.45 runs per 100 balls.

It didn't last and Durham didn't re-engage Glendenen for 1994. Not bitter, he later played for Cumberland, before becoming a security guard in Middlesbrough.

100
GREATS

David Anthony Graveney
RHB & SLA, 1992-94

David Anthony Graveney
Born: Bristol, 2 January 1953
Also played for: Gloucestershire, Somerset

Batting

M	I	NO	Runs
53	79	29	939
Ave	100	50	
18.78	0	1	

Bowling

O	Md	R	W
1,415.5	395	3,754	97
Ave	5wI	10wM	Ct
38.70	2	0	30

Best Performances
65* v. Warwickshire, 1994
6/80 v. Nottinghamshire, 1994

Durham's first first-class captain had the pedigree and experience for the job, but perhaps not the personality to meld a disparate group of personalities newly brought together.

However, David Graveney, son of Gloucestershire's Ken and nephew of Northumberland-born Tom, did use his two seasons at Durham to build his cricket CV. He progressed to the chief executive role at the Professional Cricketers' Association and, in 1997, became England's Chairman of Selectors.

Graveney was near the end of a long career as an economical and accurate slow left-armer even when he left Gloucestershire in 1990 to play for Somerset.

That year Graveney made his first contact with Durham, who applied for first-class status a year before. Graveney's made his 'big shift' after discussion with Gloucestershire's former Durham batsman Paul Romaines, who put him in touch with Durham captain Neil Riddell when Graveney said his days at Gloucestershire were numbered. Initially thinking of himself as a manager, Graveney's ban

for playing in South Africa made him only an option as a player. Geoff Cook took the Director of Cricket post while Graveney, after 10 wickets in his last Gloucestershire game (against Somerset), moved to Somerset to await Durham's next step.

Durham would have benefited from Graveney's presence earlier, and his and Cook's rebuttal of Romaines and choice of some veteran imports did not wholly win over the crowds.

Graveney said his three Durham years were his happiest in cricket. 'To be over 40 and have a fan club was remarkable,' he added, establishing the side was hard work, but 'we got there and now Durham are producing a lot of home-grown players.'

An intellectual accountant and deep thinker on the game, Graveney stayed in the Gateshead Marriott hotel during the season, leaving his wife and children in Bristol.

Graveney led Durham throughout 1992 and 1993, and although he was a likeable, genuine captain, he did not suffer fools gladly. He wrote part of the 1993 book, *Durham CCC: Past, Present and Future*, concluding with Teddy Roosevelt's words: 'Who at the best, knows in the end the triumph or high achievement, and who at the worst, if he fails, at least fails while daring greatly.'

Stephen Greensword
RHB & RM, 1970-90

Stephen Greensword			
Born: Gateshead, 6 September 1943			
Also played for: Leicestershire, Northumberland, Minor Counties			

Batting

M	I	NO	Runs
192	272	51	7,802
Ave	100	50	
35.30	7	44	

Bowling

O	Md	R	W
3,517.1	1,148	8,468	427
Ave	5wI	10wM	Ct
19.83	13	2	92

Best Performances
141* v. Cheshire, 1971
9/16 v. Cumberland, 1972

Anyone with an interest in North-East cricket will recognise the contribution all-rounder Stephen Greensword had in the 1960s, '70s and '80s.

He began with Philadelphia, moved to Leicestershire as a teenager (where he was occasionally known by the unsuitably jolly nickname of Sammy) and later played for South Shields (1971-72), Philadelphia (1973-80), Hartlepool (1981), Whitburn (1982-83), Sunderland (1984) and Eppleton (1985). Durham's Peter Pan was still appearing for Philadelphia and Durham over-fifties in 2002.

At Leicestershire, fellow all-rounder Jack van Geloven kept him out of the first team. Both subsequently played for Northumberland and later the pair met again, with Van Geloven an umpire, in Durham's 1978 GC tie against the side it vanquished five seasons before – Yorkshire. Greensword did not bowl; Chris Old bowled him for a duck and this time Durham lost, by 113 runs.

A few figures from the glory days show Greensword's consistent value. He took 27 wickets at 21.51 in 1979, scored a county record 868 at 62 in 1980 and took 21 wickets at 21.85, 501 at 35.78 in 1982 with 20 wickets at 22.65 and took 22 wickets at 20.4 in 1983.

Greensword was indeed Durham's most valuable post-war player. At the age of 26, he was signed from Northumberland in 1970 when professional at Gateshead Fell. Through his 20 years with Durham, Greensword revitalised Durham with his prolific all-round talents.

He could be free-scoring and could be dour, but always batted with correct technique. As a medium pacer he could drop the ball on a sixpence and on a juicy wicket used movement off the seam to unplayable affect. As a personality Greensword seemed miserable until he knew you well. Committed to his team, he always played hard to win, but contrastingly was keen on amateur operatics and did comedy Geordie impressions in the style of Bobby Thompson.

Durham finished third in 1971, fourth in 1972 …and won in the Gillette Cup. Greensword's performances (650 runs at 46.42 in 1971, and 43 wickets and 534 runs in 1972) were instrumental in the improvement. He took 2/19 off 12 overs in the four wicket GC win against Oxfordshire, then took 2/29 and scored a match winning 35* in the stunning 1973 GC win over Yorkshire. Durham did not do so well in the Championship and needed a century from Greensword against Northumberland to complete a seven-wicket win to clinch a GC place for 1974, with ten minutes to spare. In 1973, Greensword, playing for the Minor Counties, made his highest first-class score, 84* against West Indies at Torquay.

In 1975 he left Durham temporarily. He had played for Northumberland from 1967-69 and Durham from 1970-74, but a dispute between his club, Philadelphia, and Durham about which team was the more important for Greensword to represent kept him out of county cricket from 1975-77, when he rejoined Northumberland for a season.

Philadelphia won the Durham Senior League title six times in seven years from 1973-79. Greensword played for the club from 1973-80 and found a potent bowling partner in Stuart Wilkinson from 1975-78. Greensword scored a league record 1,274 runs in 1977, when Philadelphia regained the title after losing it the previous year to Eppleton.

Tall, slim and athletic, Greensword returned to Durham from 1978-90. With Durham's first-class status, and his own retirement close, he returned to Northumberland for two more seasons, 1991 and 1992.

In 1978 and 1979, Durham was runner-up in the Championship and in 1980 and 1981 Brian Lander's team won it. Greensword contributed in every game for the next 13 seasons. He scored 408 runs in 1979, a County Championship record of 868 in 1980 (893 at 68.69 in all) and 414 runs and 29 wickets at 17.68 in 1981.

Without an overseas player in 1982, but with Peter Kippax, who'd come to Durham from Northumberland too, Durham fell to ninth. Greensword still scored 501 runs in the Championship. In 1983 Greensword's best effort came in the NWT, when he scored 82 and took 2/40 to help beat Northumberland.

In 1984 Durham regained the Championship. The crux came against runners-up Staffordshire at Gateshead Fell, when Greensword scored 45 and 44 and took three wickets in the first innings. Needing 192 in 33 overs, Richard Mercer and Graham Johnson saw Durham home with a ball to spare. Greensword took 36 wickets at 17.66 and scored 709 runs at 39.38 – he could hardly have been asked for more.

Still contributing aged 44, he took 25 wickets at 18.88 and scored 299 runs at 29.90 in 1988.

Captain Riddell said his influence came through his dependability, and although an introvert, he offered much tactically when asked. Ashok Patel said Greensword helped his game, 'but he was one of these characters who was not well liked by those who didn't know him'.

Lance Cairns said: 'He was mean and miserable, a very limited cricketer as far as ability went, but also one of the better ones for scrapping and fighting. He had no frills, but you've got to have one in every side, who never gave their wicket away. He didn't worry if he played the whole session for 10 runs, and he'd play the cut and drive only and didn't go outside these shots. He was medium slow or slower, and bowled a little leg cutter, but did not have the pace to take wickets, so he kept the runs down to one or two an over and waited for mistakes.'

---

100 GREATS

John Gregory
RHB & OB, 1890-99

Prodigious wicket taker Jack Gregory died in obscurity in Darlington in 1935, but his record in the early years of Durham cricket lives on.

A somewhat erratic but a very useful bowler and handy aggressive batsman, Gregory's parents didn't register his birth, probably due to the expense.

Much travelled as a professional cricketer, Gregory arrived in Durham City to play as professional in 1890. He moved to Darlington from 1891-95, went back to Durham in 1896 and played for Tudhoe in 1897 and Halifax in 1899. As late as 1918 Gregory styled himself as a professional cricketer, although

John Gregory

continued

he had long since retired to become a corporation storeman.

Gregory's hard spun off breaks gave him match analyses such as 10/72 v. Lincolnshire 1895, 10/86 v. Surrey II in 1897, 10/101 v. Cambridgeshire in 1898 and 11/81 v. Worcestershire in 1895. His best match brought the best match figures for Durham, when he took 8/23 and 7/29 against Lincolnshire in 1894.

That season he took 42 wickets for the county. In 1897 he took 64, including 37 in the second-class County Championship and in 1898 he took 62 wickets, all in friendlies.

Yet he could be a poor bowler, as he strained with his pioneering arm ball or sought to spin the ball too much.

Gregory married a Darlington girl, Sarah Jane Oliver, the daughter of a builder, in 1901, and they soon had a child, christened William Gilbert.

Sadly, Gregory was buried in an unmarked grave and no death notice appeared for the once great bowler, who helped take the county successfully into its first competitive era.

John Gregory
Born: Nottingham, 1859
Died: Darlington, 1935

Batting

M	I	NO	Runs
52	73	6	71
Ave	100	50	
14.79	0	3	

Bowling

O	Md	R	W
2,014.2	726	4,167	274
Ave	5wI	10wM	Ct
15.20	25	5	32

Best Performance
9/41 v. Lincolnshire, 1895

David John Halfyard

RHB & RMF, 1971-72

David John Halfyard
Born: Winchmore Hill, 3 April 1931
Died: Northam, 23 August 1996
Also played for: Kent, Nottinghamshire, Cornwall, Minor Counties

Batting

M	I	NO	Runs
16	15	2	200
Ave	100	50	
15.38	0	1	

Bowling

O	Md	R	W
597.4	255	1,107	81
Ave	5wI	10wM	Ct
13.66	6	2	10

Best Performance
9/23 v. Staffordshire, 1971

Some cricketers can't leave the game, no matter what happens to try and drive them out. A car crash wrecked Dave Halfyard's successful county course with Kent in 1962, but he struggled back with a training programme involving running on the beach near his Mevagissey home and visiting the Kent physio hundreds of miles away.

Travel was a big factor in cricket gypsy Halfyard's career. With his whites always packed, his VW

Caravanette clocked up 317,000 miles and he played for the southernmost and northernmost Minor Counties.

Halfyard helped Durham in 1971, when he wound up as a professional for Marske, taking 33 wickets for the county. He took 48 in 1972, all but four in the Championship.

He played 185 games for Kent from 1956-64 and 77 for Nottinghamshire from 1968-70. Remarkably, he interrupted the stints with the career-threatening car crash and a year as a first-class umpire in 1967. Before putting on his white coat to umpire Nottinghamshire-Sussex at Hove in 1967, Nottinghamshire's Brian Bolus, Norman Hill and Gary Sobers spotted Halfyard practising in the nets. He won a contract with Notts and took hundreds more wickets.

For Kent, Halfyard took 100 wickets in a season five times, more than any Durham player had in first-class cricket. His best was 135 at 20.39 in 1958 and he took 9/39 against Glamorgan at Neath in 1957.

Fourteen years later, aged 41, he again had a nine-for analysis – 9/23, Durham's second best

bowling analysis, after Alf Morris' 10/130 in 1910. He also took 8/31 against Staffs in 1972 and 7/32 and 6/29 against Cumberland in the same year with his accurate medium paced cutters.

Halfyard's arrival in 1971 coincided with that of Stephen Greensword and Durham finished third and fourth in Halfyard's two seasons with the county.

He opened the bowling effectively in his two 1972 GC appearances, with figures of 12-5-11-2 in the win over Oxfordshire and 12-1-35-2, dismissing test players Younis Ahmed and Graham Roope, in the second round defeat to Surrey.

Even in his forties the more rotund Halfyard could be devastating on the right pitch, taking 10/29 for Cornwall against Dorset at Penzance in 1974.

He returned to the umpire's list in 1977, alternating spells as pro at Northumberland and Cornwall. Before his unexpected death he was bowling leg breaks for Tiverton in Devon and umpiring Devon in Minor Counties matches. Since starting with Surrey II in 1952, he had lived and breathed the game for 44 years.

Donald Wrightson Hardy
RHB & RM, 1948-67

Donald Wrightson Hardy
Born: East Boldon, 24 March 1926
Died: Felling, 17 January 1998

Batting

M	I	NO	Runs
150	205	27	3,739
Ave	100	50	
21.00	2	16	

Bowling

O	Md	R	W
2,469	238	2,469	112
Ave	5wl	10wM	Ct
22.04	4	0	90

Best Performances
132* v. Northumberland, 1955
8/31 v. Yorkshire II, 1954

Educated at Worksop College and finely schooled in the game, Don Hardy *(front row, middle)* became Mr Boldon and Mr Durham for cricket in the 1950s and 1960s.

His father Harry was a Boldon stalwart who played

for Durham in 1929-30. Don followed his father into the Boldon and Durham sides and as managing director of the family brick and tile company.

Tall and well-built, Hardy bowled unexceptional right arm medium pace and batted usefully and correctly. He made two centuries for Durham, his first being 100* *v.* Scotland in his second season, 1949. During his second, he set a Durham fifth wicket record of 178 with Malcolm Scott against Northumberland in 1955. A season earlier he took 8/31, his career best, and scored 54 out of 159 leaving Yorkshire II 308 to win. Yorkshire failed by five runs.

Hardy acceded to the Durham captaincy in 1955 and stayed there for 13 seasons. There were only five top ten finishes, but Durham did lose players such as Scott and Colin Milburn to first-class counties. Hardy retired in 1967 after becoming the

longest-serving Durham skipper.

Hardy played rugby for Sunderland in the 1940s, captained the MCCA and played for the Minor Counties against the tourists from 1958-65. Too much cricket made business suffer and Hardy later worked as a bus driver in Gateshead, living in reduced circumstances in a council flat, estranged from Boldon and Durham cricket. Sadly, he had recently been persuaded to return to Boldon CC when he died, still in relative obscurity compared to the days when he was king of all he surveyed in the county.

Stephen James Harmison
RHB & RF, 1996-date

Stephen James Harmison
Born: Ashington, 23 October 1978

Batting

M	I	NO	Runs
70	100	26	636
Ave	100	50	
8.59	0	0	

Bowling

O	Md	R	W
2,191.1	487	6,803	223
Ave	5wI	10wM	Ct
30.50	5	0	14

Best Performance
6/111 *v.* Sussex, 2001

As a 6ft 4ins gangling seventeen-year-old, Stephen Harmison made an unpromising debut in 1996, mauled by Leicestershire's Phil Simmons to return 0/77 in nine overs at the Riverside. Earlier that week Harmison had impressed by bowling future Durham coach Martyn Moxon in the Tetley Bitter Scarborough Festival semi-final. Disillusioned, and with an injured back, he returned to factory work and his beloved football with Ashington FC. Harmison missed the 1997 professional cricket season, though he managed to play for Ashington II's as a batsman. But Durham's management believed he had some bowling talent and lured him back for 1998. Harmison's pace soon stood out and England selectors noticed him, although his England touring experiences were not initially successful.

He took 49 Championship wickets at 28.57 in 1998, after only winning a year's contract shortly before the season started. Using his steep bouncer and quick yorker effectively, Harmison took 5/150, 8/102, 3/118, 3/91, 2/86 and 7/145 in the first six matches, with a best of the season of 5/70 against Gloucestershire at Chester-le-Street.

Injury forced Harmison (who dislikes being called Steve) to miss the 1999/2000 England 'A' tour to Bangladesh and New Zealand, and he admitted to homesickness when in South Africa and Zimbabwe in 1998/99. As an archetypal, good-natured northern lad, Harmison was unprepared for southern Africa and took a while to settle, even after a pre-tour team-building exercise in the Lake District.

He came good, bowling so fast (over 90mph) that third man became an attacking catcher. Harmison surpassed the injured Mel Betts and finished the tour with 5/119 off 49 overs in the match with UCBSA President's XI. Five weeks later he took 5/57 in Durham's first match of 1999, and then backed up with 7/155 in Durham's first Championship win for a year, in June against Northants. He took 25 more wickets in Durham's five further victories, including 8/100 (including former Durham captain Mike Roseberry twice) in the six-wicket win over Middlesex. In July he crusted Derbyshire's Matthew Cassar and battered the other batsmen with bouncers to butter them up for Simon Brown and Betts. He still took more wickets than them, 64 wickets at 27.73. A best of 5/76 showed his consistent, rather than dominating wicket taking.

In 2000, he made the England squad, as selectors hoped to fight West Indian bounce and pace with the same, but developed sore shins, then lost control on his return and continued his erratic form through 2001, taking four championship wickets less than 1999 in the two seasons of 2000 and 2001 put together.

Back to full fitness, Harmison spent the 2001/02 winter at the National Academy and in the summer of 2002 gained selection for the England side playing India at Trent Bridge. He had been left out at the last stage of selection several times before. Harmison went on to do so well in 2003 against Zimbabwe and Bangladesh in particular, that he had taken the sixth-most test wickets of anyone in the world (31 wickets in the eight tests) by October that year, taking 9/79, including a career best 5/35 in an easy win at Dhaka. Ironically, a back injury meant

Durham reject Martin Saggers replaced him for the last test of the 2003/04 Bangladesh series. Newspaper cricket writers repeatedly criticised what they saw as a lack of effort to return to fitness.

However Harmison did recover, helped by training with Newcastle United, to tour the West Indies in Spring 2004. By then, his fastest recorded bowling was 94mph, quicker than anyone in England and only behind a handful overseas.

Middle-class newspaper critics, generally from the south, continued to attack or ignore Harmison, until he won the Jamaica test for his country. A spell of 7/12, probably the best for England in the West Indies in a test, meant Harmison was finally recognised as the world-class bowler he had promised to be. The only possible carping could come from Durham fans, eager to see him perform for the county. Even then, their pride in Durham's finest test player was clear.

Harmison came from Jackie Milburn and the Charlton brothers' mining town. He said he found Curtly Ambrose and Courtney Walsh 'phenomenal,' and it is his similarity in style to the West Indian pair that so excited selectors.

His brothers Ben and James have both represented Northumberland and Ben joined the Durham staff in 2003.

Modest and self-effacing, Harmison said Durham's status as a first-class county was a 'great incentive for young kids looking to play cricket in the area'. Having reached the top, he said: 'it means a lot to me to walk out for Durham and give something back to the people for supporting me'.

Frank Harry
RHB & RMF, 1912-14

Frank Harry arrived at Durham from a successful county career as a professional bowler with Lancashire to help Durham and South Shields prior to the First World War.

A cricketer who occasionally achieved startling successes, Devonian Harry was a successful bowler who used movement to take wickets. He also batted a little, as in 1907 when he knocked off the 21 needed to beat Leicestershire at Blackpool in Archie McLaren's last game for Lancashire.

Always a stand-in or second fiddle at Lancashire, Harry covered for Walter Brearley, whose dispute with Lancashire's committee prevented his selection in 1906/07.

Harry's outstanding efforts for Lancashire

included 9/44 and 6/26 (15/70 in the match) against Warwickshire in 1906, 5/14 at Southbridge in 1907 and 6/18 against Leicestershire at Old Trafford in 1908. After 1911, Harry backed Harry Dean, Lancashire's strike bowler when Brearley and the committee irrevocably split.

At Durham, Harry played alongside Cecil Parkin and Alf Morris, two of Durham's finest bowlers of any era. In 1913, aged 36, after a brief debut in 1912, Harry took 48 wickets at 16.56, but still wasn't top of the averages, as Parkin, who was to debut for Lancashire the following year, took 16 wickets at 11.62. Morris took the glory with 87 wickets, his 7/71 following Harry's 7/47 in an innings win against Cambridgeshire. Harry took 7/73 in the return and the pair shared 19 wickets in the return at Ashbrooke a week later. He appeared in every match in one of Durham's strongest sides, which included Championship leading run scorer Denis Hendren, and Hugh Dales who moved to Hendren's former county Middlesex after the war.

Harry's best year came in 1914, but illness, contracted during the war, prevented him from playing on. He shared 661.2 overs with Morris in 1914, taking 44 Championship wickets and also made useful runs. However, Hendren fell away and Durham finished thirteenth after coming fifth in 1913.

In 1913, South Shields pro Harry was the bowler in the Kellet Kirtley incident, which caused a riot at Bunker Hill, as the working class Philadelphia team

clashed with middle-class South Shields. League committeemen banned inciter and Philadelphia wicketkeeper Kirtley. Harry left for peaceful sanatorium centre Malvern, playing seven matches as an amateur for Worcestershire in 1919 and 1920. He died five years later, aged 48. Harry was a publican in Malvern and coached at Malvern School, a better job than the short life of a cricket pro. He also played cricket for Cheshire and rugby for Broughton Park.

Frank Harry			
Born: Newton Abbot, 22 December 1876			
Died: Great Malvern, 27 October 1925			
Also played for: Lancashire, Worcestershire			
Batting			
M	I	NO	Runs
21	32	5	580
Ave	100	50	
21.48	0	5	
Bowling			
O	Md	R	W
613.4	144	1,678	94
Ave	5wI	10wM	Ct
17.94	7	4	7
Best Performances			
85 *v.* Glamorgan, 1914			
7/45 *v.* Northumberland, 1914			

Denis Hendren —————————————————— 100
RHB & OB, 1910-21

GREATS

Too good to leave the game, but lacking the consistency to make a county career, Denis Hendren served Durham through a difficult era either side of the First World War.

Always to be overshadowed by six years younger brother Patsy (who played for Middlesex II against Durham in 1922), Denis Hendren moved north in 1910 to pro for Durham City and made his Durham debut that year. Ian Peebles said Hendren left after 'making known his dissatisfaction' and threatening 'to look elsewhere' over being asked to stand down because a Middlesex amateur fancied a game. The Middlesex committee accepted his 'decision'. In 1911 Hendren had scored 427 at 23.72 for Durham, second in the county run scoring list behind Dick Harrison. He was professional for Burnmoor in 1913, Sunderland in 1914 and Hendon in 1921.

As a brother of one of England's greatest batsmen,

Denis suffered in comparison. While Patsy was steady, reliable and loyal, Denis was impetuous and rarely scored the runs he should, given he made four centuries for Durham. These included three (116 *v.* Cambridgeshire, 139 *v.* Cambridgeshire and 140 *v.* Lincolnshire) in 1913, more even than Elliot, one of only three pre-Second World War batsmen (Len Weight and Tom Dobson Jr were the others) to score more centuries for Durham than Hendren.

Over 15 years he played nine times for Middlesex, scoring just 109 runs and taking three wickets. In contrast Patsy, from 1907-38, scored 57,611 runs with 170 centuries, both in the top three in the first-class list. Patsy set a Middlesex partnership record with John W ('Young Jack') Hearne of 375. Altham and Swanton said in their History of Cricket: 'In the grace of execution, Hendren's homely figure could not quite match the elegance of Hearne'. But where

Denis Hendren

Born: Turnham Green, 25 September 1882
Died: London, 29 May 1962
Also played for: Middlesex

Batting

M	I	NO	Runs
45	75	3	1,853
Ave	100	50	
25.73	4	5	

Bowling

O	Md	R	W
491.1	57	1,762	70
Ave	5wI	10wM	Ct
25.17	1	0	28

Best Performances
140 v. Lincolnshire, 1913
7/82 v. Northumberland, 1913

did that leave Denis? Patsy even played top football for Brentford, Queens Park Rangers, Manchester City and Coventry City. Yet, when the Hendren's Irish immigrant parents, two brothers and sister died, Denis had taken the paternal role. Patsy said: 'I owe more than I can say to him. He was the first to catch hold of me and try to make me a cricketer. No lad had a better coach.'

So, Denis had a key role in Patsy's development. He loved cricket and kept his involvement, becoming a first-class umpire from 1931-49.

Bell said Hendren was 'at times a brilliant batsman, though a little impetuous. But for this he might never have been known in Durham cricket.'

His best year was 1913 with 738 runs at 41, including three centuries in successive games. He led the batting aggregates among the Minor Counties. Alf Morris led the wicket takers. Both appeared in every match as Durham finished fifth, but the next season Hendren's form declined and he failed to average 20.

After the war he reappeared briefly for Middlesex, and in 1921 for one more season for Durham.

100
GREATS

Dr Frederick Ironsides Herbert

LHB & LFM, 1937-50

Dr Frederick Ironsides Herbert

Born: Low Fell, 23 January 1915
Died: Gosforth, 20 February 1970

Batting

M	I	NO	Runs
26	32	16	112
Ave	100	50	
7.00	0	0	

Bowling

O	Md	R	W
576.3	109	1,608	84
Ave	5wI	10wM	Ct
19.14	3	0	10

Best Performance
6/35 v. Northumberland, 1940
(official wartime friendly)

Hickman, Harry Gibbon and Tom Dobson.

Plastic surgeon Herbert was a left arm swing operator; often unavailable because of his job, but capable of a slicing, boomerang bend when conditions were right.

Herbert played for Durham University up to 1939 while studying to be a doctor, and made his Durham debut against New Zealand in 1937, removing Walter Hadlee, Norman Gallichan, Bill Carson and Jack Lamason. It left New Zealand only 101 ahead at 41/5, before Lowry and Donnelly added 90 for the sixth wicket. Herbert took 4/29 and Durham, set 220 to win, reached a respectable 100/4 at stumps.

Austin, who couldn't play because of a broken finger, said Herbert was a dream to keep wicket to, swinging the ball in to the right hander from the edge of the crease bowling over the wicket. Hadlee remembered a left arm inswing over the wicket bowler exploiting a 'pitch that was a bit awkward. A bit of rain had fallen before we batted which made the pitch lively.'

In 1937 he played in the remaining five matches after his New Zealand debut, taking match figures of 9/50 in the win over Northumberland.

Herbert, who missed the 1939 season and moved to Benwell CC in 1940, impressed Herbert Sutcliffe

Durham's proud record against overseas touring teams reached a peak in the late 1930s. Indeed, in 1936 Durham beat All India at Ashbrooke. The following season Freddie Herbert was one of nine replacements for the likes of the ageing Albert Howell, Ellis, Charles Lodge Adamson, George

when Austin took a moral-boosting side to Catterick Garrison after the retreat from Dunkirk. After Herbert had dismissed Sutcliffe and two others at the top of the order, batting record breaker Sutcliffe (he held the first wicket stand record of 555 with Percy Holmes) said Herbert reminded him of Abe Waddington; the Yorkshire left armer who played for England in 1920/21. Herbert injured his back during D-Day operations after active service in Burma and this reduced his effectiveness, especially as a fielder. He did not play in 1946, but appeared twice more against touring teams, taking 3/80 against the Australians in 1948 and 1/66 in New Zealand's 417/3 in 1949.

Albert Louis Howell

RHB & RFM, 1926-36

100 GREATS

Like Denis Hendren, Albert Howell pursued a professional cricket career on the margins of the first-class game, eclipsed by a famous brother.

Opening bowler Albert was a Durham stalwart and professional for South Shields for eleven successful seasons (1926-36), by which time he was fourth highest wicket-taker for the county.

Howell followed elder brother Harry to Warwickshire (the family had links to Wales and Argentina) after the First World War (during which he was wounded), but failed to win a regular place in four seasons of trying. Harry took 975 wickets in 198 games for Warwickshire, carrying the attack after the war. Just as Albert could not step up to first-class level, in test cricket former Wolves and Accrington Stanley footballer Harry had a miserable time. He was on the losing team in all his first four Tests, three on the 1920/21 tour of Australia and then at Trent Bridge in the 1921 return. He won a recall against South Africa in 1924, but bowled just nine unsuccessful overs. In 1925 he told Warwick-shire he could not carry on, such was his workload, and seven years later died of illness, aged 41.

His brother, though not as good a player, had one piece of luck in his cricket career: moving to Durham. For many players Minor County cricket was the next best thing to first-class county cricket. Some preferred the less arduous Minor County circuit. Others, like Albert Howell, played at the highest level their ability allowed.

Aged 25, Howell moved north, as did Hendren and on-the-scrapheap county bowlers Frank Harry and later Alec Coxon, Ron Aspinall, Ken Biddulph, Stephen Greensword and David Halfyard.

Brummie Albert found Durham congenial to the soul. He took 40 wickets in 1928, 46 in 1929 and 48 in 1930. For Durham, only Jack Gregory, Alf Morris, Barney Anderson, John Butler, William Whitwell, and Jim Thackeray had bettered his innings figures of 8-41 (v. Northumberland 1926) and 8-36 (v. Yorkshire II 1935 aged 37). He took 12-90 against

Albert Louis Howell			
Born: Birmingham, 26 July 1898			
Died: Newcastle-upon-Tyne, 26 July 1958			
Also played for: Warwickshire			
Batting			
M	I	NO	Runs
98	122	30	1,193
Ave	100	50	
12.96	0	3	
Bowling			
O	Md	R	W
2,490.2	568	6,325	351
Ave	5wI	10wM	Ct
18.01	20	3	36
Best Performances			
73* v. Northumberland, 1929			
8/36 v. Yorkshire II, 1935			

Staffordshire and 11-51 against Yorkshire II (both 1930). In 1927 Howell was the all-round match-winner against Northumberland at Chester-le-Street taking 8-126 in the match and scoring 39 and 19, both not out in the six wicket win. He played for Minor Counties in 1929, his last first-class match.

Durham won the Minor County Championship in Howell's debut season, and in 1930. While everything was straightforward against weaker sides, against touring teams he generally struggled to take wickets. He failed to strike against Australia in 1926 and New Zealand the following season, but took 4-91 in the draw with the 1928 West Indians and 5-74 in the innings loss to South Africa in 1929. His new ball skill paid off on tougher pitches and he had South Africa 22/3, with Frank Woodhouse, the 1933 West Indians 58/8 and he shifted 1934 Australian opener Bill Brown for a duck. He even took 2/36 in the win over All India in 1936, when he ended his Minor County career with 14 wickets in the season at 22.14.

Russell Inglis
RHB & RM, 1956-73

Russell Inglis
Born: Blackhill, 13 June 1936
Died: Gosforth, 28 April 1982
Also played for: Minor Counties

Batting

M	I	NO	Runs
140	227	18	6,626
Ave	100	50	
31.70	7	39	

Bowling

O	Md	R	W
594.4	159	1,701	66
Ave	5wl	10wM	Ct
22.77	2	0	65

Best Performances
160 v. Cheshire, 1970
5/27 v. Staffordshire, 1968

Even decades after his early death Russell Inglis' *(second from right)* record still glows.

He led Durham's run scorers' list becoming the first to pass 6,000 runs. He passed 50 runs almost 50 times, but an innings of 47 had most influence on Durham's future path.

Probably Durham's best-performed batsman prior to it gaining first-class status, Inglis top scored in Durham's 1973 five wicket Gillette Cup win over Yorkshire, the first by a Minor County over a first-class county.

Inglis played his early cricket at Shotley Bridge before joining Durham City, then Chester-le-Street as a professional. He bagged a pair on his county debut, in a rare loss against Cumberland, at Keswick in 1956. It was a deceiving start, as he went on to become Durham's most prolific run scorer.

His record includes scoring a county record 500 runs in a season for Durham seven times, including 839 in 1966 and 847 in 1967 (both county records), as well as 592 in 1968, 602 in 1961, 563 in 1964, 508 in 1963, 508 in 1970 and 452 in 1962.

He represented Minor Counties against every touring team to England from 1964-69, though he never had much success against overseas sides, scoring seven when opening with David Ellis (100*) against Pakistan in 1962 in his only game for Durham against tourists.

From 1962-68 he helped Durham to seven top-ten finishes and some stirring Gillette Cup efforts. In 1967, chasing Nottinghamshire's 191/7 at Ropery Lane, 46 from Inglis took Durham to 101/2 after a partnership of 88 with Mike Westcott. However, Durham lost by 11 runs, though Inglis did rack up his

record season, with 847 runs at 44.65. His next GC contribution came four matches and 19 runs later. He made an aggressive 47 against Yorkshire, before being caught trying for a big hit off Phil Carrick at 63/2. Durham won by five wickets.

A classic Inglis effort came in 1964, when Ken Biddulph's 13/94 against Staffordshire at Darlington left Durham 85 to win. On a poor pitch, with Jack Watson's 32 the previous highest score in the match, Inglis hit 68* and Durham won by nine wickets. In 1970 against Cheshire he hit career best 160 and then made 129 out of 180 chasing a target of 219 in 199 minutes at Blackhill (where he was born within sight of the Consett CC ground), setting up one of only two wins that season, leaving thirty minutes to spare.

The increasingly stout Inglis replaced John Bailey as captain in 1972, but was not always available (Alan Old and Alan Burridge filled in) and Brian Lander took over for 1973.

Inglis scored 421 runs at 42.10 in his final season in 1973. A solid opener who had offers to join a first-class county, Inglis had outstanding club and Minor County statistics and had all the shots, being a fine driver and strong on the onside. His crafty bowling was underrated because it looked innocuous. Inglis was laidback about county cricket, preferring his own environment in the North-East, where the unpretentious cricketing gentleman worked as a fitter and turner for the Consett Iron Co.

Inglis, who never believed he was as good as player as he was, played as Chester-le-Street professional for 12 seasons (1962-73) scoring 9,911 runs at 47.75 and took 502 wickets at 13.53. His best year was 1971 with 1,200 league runs at 80. He also hit 5,035 cup runs and took 398 wickets, making a total of 14,946 runs (44.65) and 900 wickets (12.75).

Inglis suffered a heart scare during the last match of 1973 and never recovered; dying of a heart attack aged 45 in Durham CCC's centenary year.

Thomas Keith Jackson
RHB & RMF, 1947-53

Following five years as a prisoner of war in Germany, Keith Jackson returned to the North, playing cricket for Bishop Auckland and debuting for Durham in 1947, aged 29. The fast bowling all-rounder made an immediate impact, scoring 105 against Yorkshire II in his first season, adding 99 for the sixth wicket with Alan Townsend after Durham was 145/5.

His swing bowling returned two five-wicket analyses for Durham, both remarkable performances. His best bowling came against Australia in 1948, when he opened and took 5/76, bowling openers Don Tallon and Bill Brown and dismissing Neil Harvey, Ron Hamence and Lindsay Hassett. He then struck 23, before Tallon stumped him off Ian Johnson near the close of the first day. His magic game ended there as poor weather prevented play on day two. Durham was going through one of its worst spells in the Minor Counties Championship, finishing 16th in 1948 and 1949, and 21st in 1950 under Bill Proud's captaincy.

Tourist games and some fine individual performances helped make up for the lack of success. Jackson's second red-letter day came in 1950, when he became the third Durham bowler to take nine wickets or more in an innings. The other wicket was a run out.

That season he hit two of his three centuries for the county, against Yorkshire II and Northumberland. He also took 4/120 against the West Indies in 1950. His single wicket in the second innings, was Jeff Stollmeyer, caught by Arthur Austin for a

duck. Jackson had dismissed Stollmeyer lbw without scoring in the first innings. He sarcastically thanked Jackson for the pair, his first.

As a Bishop Auckland all-rounder he scored 2,960 runs and took 271 wickets. Jackson was the Barnard Castle School educated son of a Barnard Castle butcher who married into the Nimmo Castle Eden brewing family. The dapper, gentlemanly, well-spoken Jackson graduated from working as a brewery sales representative to the boardroom. He suffered from Parkinson's disease for many years before his death aged 78.

Thomas Keith Jackson
Born: Barnard Castle, 12 December 1918
Died: Castle Eden, 30 May 1997

Batting

M	I	NO	Runs
39	56	8	1,450
Ave	100	50	
30.20	3	4	

Bowling

O	Md	R	W
617	157	1,546	68
Ave	5wI	10wM	Ct
22.73	2	0	15

Best Performances
105 v. Yorkshire II, 1947
9/105 v. Yorkshire II, 1950

John Johnston
RHB & RFM, 1976-90

From Cowpen Bewley to Hartlepool (1976-82) and on to professional club cricket at Bishop Auckland, Johnny Johnston (middle) was a committed and invaluable fast bowler during Durham's run of success in the early 1980s. Indeed,

he was never on a losing side in the Championship until his seventh season with the county.

Johnston's left Chesterfield with his family at a young age. He grew up to become a pipe fitter and the quiet man of the Durham team, happy at the

John Johnston				
Born: Chesterfield, 15 February 1953				
Batting				
M	I	NO	Runs	Ave
101	39	24	85	5.66
Bowling				
O	Md	R		W
2,150.4	561	5,561		252
Ave	5wI	10wM		Ct
22.06	3	1		21
Best Performances				
6/45 v. Cambridgeshire, 1989				

end of a day of giving it his all to lean on the bar with a contented smile on his face.

He first made an impact with 4/24 in an innings win over Cumberland in his debut season, and though he rarely took wickets prolifically, he often chipped in with a few.

One of half a dozen Durham players to win three Championships, Johnston often played a supporting role for the overseas professional bowlers.

In 1981, Johnston led the averages in the campaign for a second Championship in successive years. Sometimes leading the attack in the absence of the injured Lance Cairns, he took 30 wickets at 19.93.

In Durham's 66th game since its last defeat, which was against Northumberland at Jesmond in August 1976, Johnston almost prolonged the record run still further. Against Staffordshire at Stockton in August 1982, his 4/44 could not stop Staffordshire reaching 156/8 to win by two wickets. That season he also took his then career best of

5/34 against Shropshire. In 1985, his 2/31 helped keep Derbyshire to 171 all out and set up a seven-wicket NWT win at Derby. In 1986 he took 27 wickets at 18.77 including his 150th wicket for Durham in the win over Bedfordshire.

Johnston was a consistent bowler who was loyal to his county, despite being born in Derbyshire. By 1982 he had taken 90 wickets for Durham at 22.07 and by retirement in 1990 had kept up his record, with 252 at 22.06. Johnston was a poor batsman: he scored 85 runs in 101 games for Durham.

He played 221 games for Darlington professional in the 1980s, captaining the side to the NYSD League title as an amateur in 1990, when he won the league's best amateur award. In 1988, Surrey and Lancashire bowler Tony Murphy replaced the injured Johnston for a game against Hartlepool at Feethams, taking 0/93 and scoring two in his sole appearance.

Johnston later lived at Norton and was a keen spectator at Durham games.

Dean Mervyn Jones
RHB, 1992

Durham's first, and best, overseas import, Dean 'The Legend' Jones, could have served the county well throughout the 1990s.

However, he stayed just one season, setting records for highest Championship and first-class average, most centuries, most Sunday League runs, highest Sunday score, and highest first-class score. Nationwide, he was third in the first-class averages, and first in the Sunday League averages, with second most runs, behind Desmond Haynes.

Durham captain David Graveney and Director of

Cricket Geoff Cook selected Jones ahead of Richie Richardson as overseas player for 1992. Jones proved to be a wise choice, despite his limited availability due to Australia's tour of Sri Lanka, which began in August.

The brutally opinionated, larger than life Jones was looking to improve his technique in the UK. Playing for Victoria in the 1991 Champions' Challenge against Essex, then in a friendly against Durham, Jones' confidence and positive approach impressed Graveney. Critics had found Jones

Dean Mervyn Jones
Born: Coburg, Australia, 24 March 1961
Also played for: Victoria, Australia, Derbyshire

Batting

M	I	NO	Runs
14	23	7	1,179
Ave	100	50	Ct
73.68	4	5	12

Best Performance
157 v. Northamptonshire, 1992

bumptious, cocky and arrogant, but, aged 31, the man who once led Victoria out to field wearing short trousers was keen to give Durham his all in 1992.

Jones' best score came after a shortage of early season luck. Curtly Ambrose dropped him and he was last out for 157 out of 253, leaving Northants 92 to win off nine overs. Allan Lamb and Alan Fordham got them. Such were the frustrations of Durham's last place finish in its first season. Jones also hit a 154* against Nottinghamshire which saved the game, but during the innings he damaged his finger. It ended his season and he flew home to Australia six weeks before the end of the season to recover for his trip to Sri Lanka.

A fierce hooker, unusually quick runner between the wickets and assured deep fielder, the too honest for his own good Jones became a hero with the Durham crowds second only to Botham.

An incessant talker, 'Deano', who had won fame in cricket circles for his bravery after ending up on a drip following his 210 at a hot Madras in 1987, had mixed fortunes with England tours. He failed to win selection for the 1985 tour, but topped the averages in 1989, scoring 1,510 runs at 88, including two test centuries and 248 against Warwickshire. Jones scored 1,000 test runs in 1989, scored centuries in both innings of a Test against Pakistan in January 1990 and was a mainstay in the Australia Test and one day middle order. In the 1991/92 Sheffield Shield, Jones scored 1,248 runs at 96, but came to Durham off the back of the loss of the home World Cup in February/March 1992.

He eased Durham into the Championship in 1992, advising and encouraging younger players. 'A great inspiration to the players,' said Graveney, of a player who 'made my job as a captain a lot easier.'

However, Jones' stay at Durham was ultimately unsuccessful – selectors overlooked him for the 1993 tour to England.

John George Keeler

RHB & RM, 1942-57

100 GREATS

South Moor is a small and proud club formed around 1882, which plays in the North West Durham League. Jackie Keeler, the club's finest product was also small and proud, and during his decade and a half with Durham, played some of the noblest innings for the county.

'As a small boy, my grandfather used to always say to me that if every country on earth had played cricket, there would have been no wars,' Keeler wrote in the introduction to A History of South Moor Cricket Club. However, Germany didn't play cricket and war interrupted Keeler's early progress, though he played for the Royal Navy and Combined Services.

John George Keeler
Born: South Moor, 2 May 1924

Batting

M	I	NO	Runs
62	93	4	2,393
Ave	100	50	Ct
26.88	4	10	19

Best Performance
135 v. India (at Ashbrooke), 1952

In 1946/47, Keeler, a colliery keeker, helped South Moor to the Tyneside Senior League Division A Championship. Keeler thought of playing for Northumberland, and had trials with Warwickshire and Leicestershire, but settled at Durham, and at Benwell in the Northumberland League, where he was professional from 1949-52.

The innings for which he is remembered came during this period. Against the West Indies in 1950, he scored 90 and 97 at Ashbrooke. While Sonny Ramadhin only bowled three overs and Alf Valentine was not playing, Keeler's runs came out of Durham's 366 over two innings. The next highest

Durham score was fellow opener Jim Clarke's 39, made in the second innings when the West Indies captain, John Goddard used nine bowlers in 50 overs.

Strong cutter Keeler scored 109 in the county first wicket record of 215 v. Yorkshire II with Harry Bell (113) in 1952. In July of same season he followed his two 90s against the West Indies with 135 (out of 302/6 declared) against India at Ashbrooke. After adding 128 with Alec Coxon for the second wicket, Durham was 200/1, but cranky Coxon and captain Bill Proud were both run out, which probably made Keeler want to stay in the middle as long as possible. George Crawford said Keeler was renowned for his stickability, graft and doggedness in the middle.

'Chipper' Keeler, who scored 10 and one for the Minor Counties against the Australians in 1953, shifted to Burnmoor for 1953-54 and to Chester-le-Street from 1955. Renowned for his strong wrists, quick feet and good timing, he scored two and eight against South Africa, bowled by Neil Adcock, then caught off Viv Smith in Durham's unflattering innings and 324 run defeat in the 1955 game, his last. Later confined to a wheelchair, Keeler still watched Durham matches into his seventies and had strong memories of his playing days.

100 GREATS

Neil Killeen
RHB & RMF, 1995-date

Durham's seam attack in the late 1990s was second to no other county. Simon Brown played for England, Melvyn Betts and Stephen Harmison for England 'A', John Wood had been there forever; Martin Saggers was surplus to requirements. But the most reliable bowler, when fit, was Neil Killeen, who made the Durham side in 1995 when working on a sports science degree at the University of Teesside.

'Killer' Killeen, a deep thinker about the game, was athletic enough as a teenager to represent English Schools in the javelin, though his fitness often let him down later. He won his first Durham call-up in place of the injured John Wood for the pre-1992 tour of Zimbabwe, when his father Glen had to queue up in Glasgow for the schoolboy's first passport.

In 1995 he showed promise with 5-26 against Northamptonshire in the Sunday League, the first Durham five-for in the competition. Killeen's one-day contribution, always at least as good as anyone else's, peaked with another record, 6-31 against Derbyshire at Derby in the 2000 NL.

Killeen, who always knew his figures as he walked off, played just four Championship games altogether in 1997 and 1998, missing out on the Riverside seam bonanza. Perhaps lucky to avoid the end of season player cull, he got into shape replaced injured Betts and kick-started his Durham career in June 1999. Using his new out swinger, he took 6/20 and scored 45 to add 87 for the eighth wicket with Shotley Bridge compatriot Paul Collingwood at Northampton to give Durham its first Championship win for a year. He finished with 58 wickets at 18.44, ending the season with 4/62 and 4/57 in the promotion-gaining win over Warwickshire and 7-85 against Leicestershire at Leicester, in David Boon's last match.

In 2000 an early injury meant just twenty-two Championship victims, while in 2001 he was frustrated again with just seven wickets in three matches. In 2002, 6ft 2in Killeen became the first Durham bowler to take 100 wickets in the one-day league, during a season when he took 30 wickets (a Durham record 43 in all one-dayers), including 4/12 against Leicestershire. His accurate at the death one-day value was emphasised by the three wickets he took in the final over of a National

Neil Killeen
Born: Shotley Bridge, 17 October 1975

Batting

M	I	NO	Runs
71	104	21	917
Ave	100	50	
11.04	0	0	

Bowling

O	Md	R	W
1,968.5	496	5,949	202
Ave	5wI	10wM	Ct
29.45	7	0	19

Best Performance
7/70 v. Hampshire, 2003

League game at Derby in 2000, which prevented Derbyshire scoring the six runs needed for victory. By 2003, Killeen had taken more than 200 wickets in both one day and first-class cricket.

He is a coach in the off-season and employs former team mate Martin Speight in his coaching schools.

Thomas Kinch ———————————————— 100
RHB, 1906-26   GREATS

A loyal committeeman and Durham captain in the difficult post-First World War years, Tom Kinch was also the batsman who gave Durham its reputation as worthy opposition for touring teams.

He scored 105 v. Australian Imperial Forces in 1919, Durham's first century against overseas opposition. Hon. Secretary William Bell said in 1931: 'It is possible that this match has had more to do with the placing of Durham in its present high position than any other event in the club's history.' There had been hesitation from counties to play the Australians, due to doubts about strength, but Durham's drawn game at West Hartlepool was such a hospitable success that Australia, including 1919 players Herbie Collins, Johnny Taylor and Bertie Oldfield, (and Nip Pellew and Jack Gregory who didn't play) returned in 1921. Kinch, as captain, scored 38 (out of 168) and nought in a 10-wicket loss. The Australians came back four more times, in 1926, 1934, 1938 and 1948, each time to Ashbrooke.

Correct bat and outstanding cover fielder Kinch had served in France with the 19th Durham Light Infantry during the First World War. He'd played

Thomas Kinch
Born: Darlington, 1884
Died: Swillington

Batting

M	I	NO	Runs
74	128	11	2,843
Ave	100	50	Ct
24.29	2	13	22

Best Performance
107 v. Northumberland, 1919

for Durham since 1906, under Edgar Elliot, then Tom Coulson, Charles Young Adamson and Ernest Proud, whom he succeeded in 1920.

In 1919 the West Hartlepool club player scored 379 runs for Durham at 54.12 and represented the Minor Counties against the MCC at Lord's in a non first-class match.

Kinch succeeded Ernest Proud as Durham captain in 1920. Durham was going through a fallow spell and when the county came twentieth in 1924 Kinch resigned, though he played ten more games in three years under new skipper Bertie Brooks, always reappearing for the tourist fixture, playing his seventh and final tourist match in seventeen years against Australia in 1926. Kinch and Brooks were the sole survivors of the pre-war Durham team. By 1926, Kinch, and the 41 year old

Brooks, were the only ones old enough to remember the 1901 Championship-winning side when Kinch helped Durham in two games 25 years later to its next title.

Kinch, who also played for Durham County Pilgrims represented Durham and Seaton Carew at golf. He was a shipowner's clerk who later lived in Tadcaster.

100
GREATS

Peter Kippax
RHB & LB, 1978-90

The miserly Yorkshire character never welcomed the flamboyant leg spinner, which in Peter Kippax's case, was Durham's gain.

He played four times for Yorkshire in 1961-62, taking eight wickets and scoring 37 runs. Like his father, Horace and son Simon, he wasn't to make it at first-class level, but he nevertheless performed with skill in second eleven, club and Minor County cricket.

Brian Lander, Durham captain in Kippax's first two seasons at the county, said Kippax was as aggressive as a quick bowler but retained his control.

Kippax came to Durham from Northumberland, like Stephen Greensword, with whom he had toured Kenya in the Minor Counties team of 1977/78. Neil Riddell, Durham's new captain was on the tour too, and Kippax, Hartlepool's professional, joined Durham, which came second in the Championship for the second year in succession. He scored his only Durham century that year and recorded his best bowling figures to date, 5/25 against Shropshire. Kippax also took 3/64 against Yorkshire in the 1978 GC loss. Bowling with players like Greensword, Wasim Raja, Johnny Johnston, Stuart Wilkinson and Lance Cairns, Kippax rarely had the chance to clean up, but he consistently took wickets and contributed with the bat.

Kippax, who usually wore a hat to hide his wrapover hairstyle starred in the Championship winning years of 1980 and 1981. He was one of the early sledgers who used to say 'come and hit my apples from the sky' to naïve batsmen, who often stepped down the wicket and were stumped by Richard Mercer. Nevertheless, Kippax was a gentleman off the pitch.

In 1987 he took 24 wickets at 15.67 in the Championship, but the following season, aged 47 and after a shoulder operation, his career looked finished, although he returned for a final fling in 1990. He played his last first-class match, for the

Peter Kippax
Born: Huddersfield, 15 October 1940
Also played for: Yorkshire, Northumberland

Batting

M	I	NO	Runs
74	78	23	1,183
Ave	100	50	
21.50	1	3	

Bowling

O	Md	R	W
1,527.3	499	3,747	192
Ave	5wl	10wM	Ct
19.51	6	0	16

Best Performances
124* v. Devon, 1978
5/23 v. Cambridgeshire, 1990

MCC, in 1987, a quarter of a century after debuting for Yorkshire.

Kippax later recommended John Wood to Durham and assisted the county in the change to first-class status after retiring in 1990, coaching young bowlers with Chris Old in 1992 and 1993.

Lance Cairns said: 'Any team is going to need someone to bowl a side out. Being a leg spinner he was going to be a wicket taker. He could rip it, and we could afford to carry Kippy in the sense he might be a bit expensive. I faced him a couple of times in club games and he knew I could slog it, but would still attack and only put a couple on the boundary. Batting he was no slug either, his fielding was a liability, but he was a great team man.' Stuart Wilkinson said, not unreasonably, Kippax was: 'One of the best leg spinners in the world at that time.'

Kippax worked in his bat-making business and coached cricket at Woodhouse Grove School.

James Thomas 'Kellet' Kirtley

RHB & WK, 1899-1908

James Thomas 'Kellet' Kirtley				
Born: Philadelphia, 1874				
Died: Ryhope, 1949				
Batting				
M	I	NO	Runs	
84	125	17	1,390	
Ave	100	50	Ct	St
12.87	0	3	65	51
Best Performance				
83 *v.* Lancashire II, 1906				

Scourge of umpires, James 'Kellet' Kirtley was a legendary figure for Philadelphia in the DSCL and Durham at the turn of the century.

He once straight drove 120 yards into road outside Bunker Hill ground, and with no long stop, squatted so close to the bails his moustache would knock them off.

Keeping wicket, Kirtley once lost two teeth to a fast ball from Ernie Liddle, and collapsed a few overs later after admonishing batsman Revd William Law, the Eppleton captain (and Durham committeeman from 1913 and Hon. Secretary 1935-52), for his poor batting, which he said caused the injury.

Albert Howell once found the shoulder of Kirtley's bat; the ball looped up and Kirtley smacked it out of ground. Howell appealed, Kirtley stood his ground, but his partner, the Revd Cecil Booth persuaded him to go, 'but not for that bugger of an umpire'.

Kirtley, for all his eccentricities, was a very good wicketkeeper, 'probably with (Johnny) Common (79 catches and 53 stumpings for Durham) and (Tom) Lambert, (56/35) the best who have given the county any length of service,' said Hon. Secretary William Bell.

Intemperate Kirtley worked at Lady Dorothea Colliery where 'Big Man' and chairman of Philadelphia CC James Pallister shifted Kellett from the pit to a colliery house maintenance job. Pallister bought Kellet two pints before each home game, at the Lambton Castle pub, which was run by colliery bosses.

On 31 August 1912 South Shields, a club made up from the professional classes, met Philadelphia's pitmen. Ten weeks earlier Shields had bowled Philadelphia out for 11, a competition record low. The scene was set for a clash and when Shields professional Frank Harry bowled Philadelphia's last man, and the bail toppled, bedlam broke out, as some players said Shields' wicketkeeper Harry Ellis had knocked the bail off. Under barrage of stones led by Kirtley, the Shields dressing room was besieged, until Philadelphia's players fled.

Philadelphia were fined a guinea and two points, Kirtley was banned for life from the League and Bunker Hill ground, though before the start of the 1914 season prohibitions lifted. Kirtley played on until he was fifty with Durham Coast League side Ryhope, where he lived.

William Kennedy Laidlaw

RHB & RLB, 1948-52

Bill Laidlaw was the finest spinner to play for Durham. Jack Bannister said the Edinburgh veteran was the 'best specialist slow bowler ever to play for the county,' and Laidlaw proved his worth by taking an average of five wickets a game in his five seasons at Durham.

Educated at Edinburgh Institute, the balding, bespectacled Laidlaw played 15 games for Scotland either side of the war and two for Minor Counties in 1950. His best bowling was 7/70 against

Yorkshire at Harrogate on his first-class debut in 1938. Formerly of the Melville College FP and Grange clubs, Laidlaw, of medium height and build, moved to Philadelphia from 1948-51 and on to Sunderland in 1952.

He took 47 wickets in 1948, and 57 in 1949, both times heading the Durham attack. However, the county finished 16th, 16th and 22nd in his first three seasons, despite analyses such as 10/106 against Staffordshire in 1948, 12/65 *v.* Northumberland in

William Kennedy Laidlaw
Born: Edinburgh, 26 August 1912
Died: 1993
Also played for: Scotland, Minor Counties

Batting

M	I	NO	Runs	Ave
31	35	9	227	8.73

Bowling

O	Md	R	W
858.3	168	2,621	166
Ave	5wI	10wM	Ct
15.78	15	5	9

Best Performance
8/45 v. Cheshire, 1951

1948 and 8/98 in an innings v. Northumberland in 1948. He also took 11/151 v. Staffordshire in 1949, 12/140 v. Northumberland 1949, and 12/134 v. Cheshire in 1951 including 8/45 in the second innings.

In 1950 Laidlaw played for Minor Counties v. West Indies at Norwich with Durham's Harry Bell. In 1951, he topped the averages ahead of new former Yorkshire players Ron Aspinall and Alec Coxon, with 30 wickets at 9.46 as Durham won four out of eight games to leap to fourth in the table.

However, the tourists generally gave him hammer. Australia's Keith Miller got to him in 1948 – Laidlaw took 1/90 off 16.5 overs – and Verdun Scott, Brun Smith and Frank Mooney did so during his 1/105 off 22 overs against New Zealand in 1949. On the same tour Laidlaw took 4-123 in 21 overs for Scotland v. New Zealand, before finally bowling chief punisher Bert Sutcliffe for 183, 23 boundaries. He also returned 2/76 off 15 overs and 0/52 off six v. West Indies in 1950. He didn't play against India in 1952, his last season for Durham.

100
GREATS

Brian Richard Lander
RHB & RM, 1963-82

Brian Richard Lander
Born: Bishop Auckland, 9 January 1942
Also played for: Minor Counties

Batting

M	I	NO	Runs
105	95	25	919
Ave	100	50	
12.94	0	1	

Bowling

O	Md	R	W
1,622.3	379	4,389	192
Ave	5wI	10wM	Ct
22.85	6	0	55

Best Performances
56 v. Cheshire, 1977
6/31 v. Bedfordshire, 1984

Captaincy brought out the best in Brian Lander and when leading Durham in the big games he was better still.

On 30 June 1973, Lander won national fame for shooting out Yorkshire's Richard Lumb, Jack Hampshire, Richard Hutton, Phil Carrick and Tony Nicholson as he led Durham to a Minor County's first victory over first-class opposition in the Gillette Cup. This set up Durham's best era in the early 1980s, and started the momentum towards Durham's elevation to first-class status.

Lander won the Man of the Match award from Cyril Washbrook for his 5/15, by far his best performance for Durham. Removing Hampshire and Hutton in successive deliveries left Yorkshire 49/5 on the way to 135 all out.

Lander's leadership from 1973-79 was a valuable part of Durham's success, particularly in winning the 1976 Championship and the trio of runners-up finishes from 1977-79.

Lander played for Durham City throughout his twenty-year Durham career. He had played 20 times for Durham in 10 years before he replaced the ill Inglis as captain in 1973. He played just nine times up to 1972, when, aged 30, he took 2/46 and 3/36 in the GC games against Oxfordshire and Surrey and played 11 out of 12 Championship games. He had switched from leg spin to medium pace leg cutters in the mid-sixties and produced many useful, if rarely devastating, performances in the 1970s. Tall, he bowled with bounce and could change his pace without changing his action.

After 1973 the county committee congratulated Lander on the team spirit and his popularity. In 1974 and 1975, Lander said the unsettled side made things difficult, but when Mohinder Armanath signed up for 1976, Durham began its best era.

Steve Atkinson, Stuart Wilkinson and Lander's Durham City team mate Richard Mercer formed the team's backbone. Lander said he didn't need to discipline players, and with a few quiet words helped form a team identity. He retired as captain after 1979 when he had an elbow operation, but returned to play until 1982. He later took a committee role until the county became first-class.

Lance Cairns said: 'Brian was a gentleman. He always played nice cricket – you were not going to get sledging with Brian. He was old school really.

David O'Sullivan compared Lander to Hampshire's Charterhouse and Oxford University educated Richard Gilliat, his captain at Hampshire: 'Although he was not a brilliant player – he bowled a bit, and smacked the ball around a bit down the order, he a very good captain.'

Lander, whose father was a policeman, was a computer technician at Durham University for many years.

Wayne Larkins

RHB & RM, 1992-95

Wayne Larkins
Born: Roxton, 22 November 1953
Also played for: Northamptonshire, England, Eastern Province, Bedfordshire

Batting

M	I	NO	Runs
67	120	6	4,278
Ave	100	50	
37.52	10	20	

Bowling

O	Md	R	W	Ct
11	1	61	0	62

Best Performance
158* v. Gloucestershire, 1994

Wayne Larkins became a sad figure in retirement after his years of audacious batting came to a close. A carefree figure at Northamptonshire for twenty years, with a justified reputation as one of England's most attractive opening batsmen, Larkins sought a new challenge at Durham in 1992. It was like the ghost of Colin Milburn coming home when the nonchalant, entertaining, attacking beer-and-cigarettes figure of Larkins moved north.

He set records for the county, for most runs in a season (1,536 in 1992), most centuries in a season (four, a record shared with Dean Jones in 1992), most career centuries (10) and highest scores in all three one-day competitions.

Recorded in Nottingham's County FC's books, Larkins, as a teenager, missed a 1987 test recall because of a football injury. He returned, at captain

Graham Gooch's request, eight and a half years after six tests in 1980 and 1981 on the 1989/90 tour of West Indies. But while Gooch's career peaked around 1990-91, Larkins' test recall lasted just seven matches, so when he made his Durham debut he was a has-been just fifteen months after his final test.

It didn't seem to worry 'Ned,' who was still capable of bold and destructive batting. However, consistency eluded him more than ever. But money worried him more. Gambling and drinking expenditure wrecked Larkins' career.

A typical Ned story came in 1992 when Durham drew the plumb trip to Dublin in the NWT. The Irish traditionally used to lay on plenty to eat and drink for opposing players, while taking it easy on the day before the game themselves. Larkins and Ian Smith got stuck in at the bar when told their rooms weren't ready on arrival at the hotel at 10 a.m.. Larkins eventually had to be carried upstairs by injured Ian Botham, who was there as a non-playing 'chaperone' and Dean Jones, before the evening do had even started. Mild-mannered captain David Graveney went ballistic, but Larkins could not be roused and was threatened with the sack. The next

day, after turning up at ten to eleven, he promised Graveney he would not only perform, but also hit the first two deliveries straight for six. He did. Most of the way through his 113, Larkins said to umpire David Shepherd that he hadn't yet seen a ball. But that was the way Larkins played.

It caught up in his last season, 1995. Larkins scored 737 runs at 32.04. Against Leicestershire his famous 'piece of piss' comment arose from a going over by quickie David Millns. Nerveless Larkins narrowly avoided several 'flesh-seeking lifters' (Simon Hughes) before spanking Millns to the fence and giving nightwatchman Hughes his well-known summation.

He hit 112 against Northamptonshire to complete the full set of centuries against all seventeen counties, but typically celebrated too hard and fell over when inspecting the wicket before the next morning's Sunday League game after picking up his mother Mavis, who wanted to watch Wayne bat. He scored a century in his last innings for Durham, but Geoff Cook had decided to sack his former opening partner and Larkins drifted out of the only job he could do via Bedfordshire and Leamington Spa CC. He was later a milkman.

Clive William Leach
RHB & SLA, 1959-65

Clive William Leach
Born: Bombay, India, 4 December 1934
Also played for: Warwickshire, Buckinghamshire

Batting

M	I	NO	Runs
66	101	7	2,006
Ave	100	50	
21.34	0	8	

Bowling

O	Md	R	W
1,076	279	2,826	145
Ave	5wI	10wM	Ct
19.48	6	2	69

Best Performances
98 v. Cumberland, 1964
6/9 v. Staffordshire, 1959

sional. However, on his return to the North in the early 1970s he made a much greater impact than as a professional cricketer – as a television executive.

Like Norman Owen before and Williamson after, Clive Leach left an unfulfilled county career to become Bishop Auckland club profes-

The half-Indian Leach took 71 wickets and scored 744 runs in his first season at Bishop Auckland (1959) and continued with Bishops as

an amateur from 1962. He scored 3,730 runs and took 287 wickets before moving to Little Chalfont in Buckinghamshire, where he played after 1965 for the county and the Amersham club.

He recommended hard-hitting all-rounder Bill Blenkiron to Warwickshire in 1964. Blenkiron had 11 seasons at the county before returning to Bishops as pro. His son, Darren, also represented Durham before an incident when he scratched two club cars led to his sacking. Leach's Durham career lasted almost twice as long as his first-class stint.

Leach scored 556 runs for Durham in 1959 and shared 86 wickets with Jack Watson, although the county finished 19th in the table. He followed first innings figures of 6/9 in 13.2 overs on a turning pitch at Gateshead Fell with 6/40 in the second innings, taking Durham to an innings and 46 run win over Staffordshire, one of only three wins that year.

He opened against India at the end of his first season with Durham, scoring 22 (adding 67 with Milburn) and 24. He took 2/30 in another draw against tourists from the subcontinent at Ashbrooke,

when Middlesbrough opener David Ellis scored a century against Pakistan.

In 1961 Leach captained Durham five times in the absence of Hardy. Though not required to bowl, Leach, with 27*, the highest score of the match at Feethams, hit the winning runs in Durham's first GC victory, against Hertfordshire in 1964. After one more season in the North, he played for Buckinghamshire for five seasons until 1971.

Leach, a CBE, ran Yorkshire and Tyne Tees Television in 1992/93 and worked for the company for 30 years in all. He lives near Tadcaster. In 2001, the Government appointed him chairman of Yorkshire Cultural Consortium. His public and professional roles have included fellowship of the Royal Society of Arts, membership of the Chartered Institute of Marketing, the executive chairmanship of Yorkshire Enterprise Ltd and its subsidiary, Yorkshire Fund Managers Ltd, the chairmanship of Gabriel Communications, a publishing company, and chairmanship of West Yorkshire Learning and Skills Council.

Jonathan James Benjamin Lewis ——— 100
RHB & OB, 1997-date

Jonathan James Benjamin Lewis
Born: Isleworth, 21 May 1970
Also played for: Essex

Batting

M	I	NO	Runs
110	198	10	6,247
Ave	100	50	Ct
33.22	11	37	46

Best Performance
210* v. Oxford University, 1997 (Durham debut)

A century on his Essex debut wasn't enough to give combative opener Jon Lewis a regular place. A double-hundred in his first game for Durham led to permanent selection in a weak batting side, where he contended with the home pitch, lack of support and the captaincy to often lead Durham's batting.

Lewis' 116* in Essex's final Championship game of 1990 promised much and his Durham record 210*, in Boon's first match as captain, more. He played decisive innings in Durham's two Championship victories that season (1997), carrying his bat for 158 against Kent and scoring 160* against Derbyshire, topping the Durham averages with 1,034 Championship runs at 39.76.

However, second season blues hit in 1997 with 578 runs at 23.12, a fall to ninth in the averages. Yet in 1999 he topped the list again, leading the run scoring in four-day (1,146 at 40.92) and one-day cricket. It was back to square one in 2000, with 645 runs at 24.80. After captain Nick Speak lost the confidence of some players as Durham struggled post-Boon, Vice Captain Lewis took over for the last two Championship games. He declared at 39/1 in the second innings against Hampshire, who scored 292/4 to win. Then champions Surrey won by an innings at The Oval.

Strong and short (the 5ft 9in batsmen was nicknamed Mini-Me after the Austin Powers film character), Lewis said of his Essex career: 'I was like a squad player at a football team.' Durham struck Lewis as a 'progressive, very professional set-up,' so he moved north. He said: 'I always fancied myself as a captain,' having played under Keith Fletcher, Graham Gooch and David Boon. 'Proud and honoured to be asked to captain this ambitious club,' Lewis had much to do to regain team faith in 2001. Known by some as Himmler, he topped the one-day averages (scoring 639 runs) and scored 890 runs at 28.90 with centuries against Nottinghamshire (adding a Durham Championship record of 258 with Martin Love) and Worcestershire, as well against Durham UCCE in its first-class bow. Down the order he scored 76* off 66 balls against Worcestershire to clinch promotion in the final NUL match.

In 2003, Lewis had his best season, passing John Morris' Durham run scoring record whilst hitting seemingly endless half-centuries in the early season plus a single century in the win over Yorkshire. However, Durham, and Lewis, tailed off in late summer.

Lewis, whose father Graham played county schools cricket, studied at King Edward VI School in Chelmsford, for a BSc (Hons) in Sports Science at Roehampton Institute and qualified as a NCA senior coach.

100 GREATS

John Wilton Lister
RHB, 1983-88

John Wilton Lister
Born: Darlington, 1 April 1959
Also played for: Derbyshire

Batting

M	I	NO	Runs
62	96	7	2,717
Ave	100	50	Ct
30.52	3	15	39

Best Performance
132 v. Bedfordshire, 1986

Listeria hit Feethams when stand-in keeper John Lister caught the first six Thornaby batsmen when regular Andy Fothergill was unavailable for the last game season 1983.

Educated at Darlington at Hummersknott Comprehensive, Lister had three seasons at Derbyshire from 1978-80, beginning his first-class career with an all run four.

He failed to make the Championship team in his last year, but had hopes of a contract extension after scoring 209, a Derby II record, against Northants II in August 1980. After the game, he was told that his contract was not to be renewed, and after playing for Worksop and West Hallam whilst at the county, he moved to Elland in Yorkshire for 1981. He had shoulder surgery on his return to Feethams in 1982. In 1984 he broke Frank Smith's 55 year old league record with 1,112 runs and also reached 1,000 in 1987 and 1988. He was Darlington captain from 1985, when Darlington won the NYSD league.

A good bat when set but a sticky starter, slow talker Lister scored a century in his third game for Durham in 1983 against Norfolk at Chester-le-Street. In 1984 Lister (87) added a quick 137 for the third wicket with Stephen Greensword to set up a tight win over Cambridgeshire as Durham went on to win the Championship.

The following season Lister, a fine close to the wicket fielder, gained his revenge over former employers Derbyshire by scoring 42 as opener in the historic second win by the county over first-class opposition in the one-day competition. Durham also won the English Estates knockout.

Lister scored well in 1986 and 1987, finishing his Minor County career in 1988, aged just 28. He joined the family business as a successful fruit and vegetable seller on Darlington market.

Martin Lloyd Love ———————————————
RHB & OB, 2001-03

Martin Lloyd Love
Born: Munduberra, Australia, 30 March 1974
Also played for: Australia, Queensland

M	I	NO	Runs
28	50	3	2,718
Ave	100	50	Ct
57.83	4	19	32

Best Performance
273 *v.* Hampshire, 2003

Durham's overseas imports ranged from the unqualified success of Dean Jones in 1992, to the relative failure of Sherwin Campbell in 1996. Andy Cummins and Manoj Prabhakar had reasonable returns, but the members' feeling was that Australians, like Jones, David Boon and Simon Katich were the most reliable signings.

Only signed when Katich made the 2001 Australian squad to tour England, Love hit 61 and 67 on his Championship debut and 14 fifties in the season. He made a single century, but contributed much at slip and with his dedication, scoring 1,364 first-class runs at 50.51 in all.

In 2002, Love returned made a duck, then 101* against Middlesex, then six weeks later 251, mostly stroked along the ground against the same county at Lord's, helping Durham to 645/6 declared, its highest score. Laidback Love drove Phil Tufnell to distraction, and the volatile England spinner eventually chucked the toys out of the pram. A broken finger then ended Love's season.

On his comeback he was one of three Durham players involved in the 2002/03 Ashes series when Love made his test debut with Stephen Harmison and Paul Collingwood in England's 12. He scored double centuries for Queensland and Australia 'A' against England in 2002/03, leading to his test debut, replacing injured Darren Lehmann for the Boxing Day match at the MCG.

Love made his Queensland debut in the 1992/93 Sheffield Shield final, and the correct, elegant, tall, assured No.3 has been in four first-class title winning sides and two Mercantile Mutual/ING Cup winning teams, scoring centuries in the first two Shield finals. The 6ft 1in batsman toured England in 1995 with Young Australia, but missed most of the 1996-97 season due to a knee reconstruction and had to wait to 2001 for national recognition when he won one of the 25 elite Australian Cricket Board contracts. In 2003 he again broke the Durham individual innings record, though he was unavailable for much of the season and Javagal Srinath, Shoaib Akhtar, Dewald Pretorius took up the overseas berths. In 2003, Australian international also-rans Brad Hodge (once briefly of Durham), Mike Hussey and Murray Goodwin all matched Love in breaking county innings bests. Love also scored his maiden test century in 2003, against Bangladesh. In November that year, he won a spirit of Anzac medal for hitting Queensland's first triple century – though he could not win a regular test place.

Quieter than the average Australian, but respected in the dressing room, 'Handles' qualified as a physiotherapist at the University of Queensland. Umpires regard him as a class act, who plays with time to spare, generally in front of the wicket.

Richard Henry Mallett ———————————————
RHB & RM, 1894-1906

When second-class counties still had to arrange fixtures amongst themselves, remote Durham almost folded due to lack of matches. Harry Mallett surmounted the problems of money and travel to help the county survive and prosper.

The greatest difficulty the club experienced for several years after formation in 1882 was the securing of fixtures. So in December 1886 Mallett attended the county representatives meeting at Lord's to arrange matches for 1887. As well as home and away matches against Northumberland and

Richard Henry Mallett
Born: Louth, 14 October 1858
Died: Ickenham, 29 November 1939
Also played for: Marylebone Cricket Club

Batting

M	I	NO	Runs
44	69	3	1,032
Ave	100	50	
15.63	1	4	

Bowling

O	Md	R	W
196.1	52	478	23
Ave	5wI	10wM	Ct
20.78	2	0	33

Best Performances
109 v. Cambridgeshire, 1897
7/94 v. Sussex, 1888

Cumberland, Mallett arranged fixtures with the Canadians and Harrow Wanderers, both at Durham. Mallett attempted to attract Lancashire to Durham for 1888, but failed. In December 1890 Durham, led by Mallett, initiated action to classify counties and begin promotion on merit. In late 1894 Mallett entered the new second-class County Cricket Championship on Durham's behalf. Durham shared the inaugural title with Norfolk. Difficulties with fixtures continued, but by 1898 Mallett had persuaded first-class counties to enter second XIs in the competition, which began to take off.

Mallett was Durham captain in 1897, when he made his top score 109, his only century for the county. He showed that the pressures of captaincy did not worry him, scoring 283 runs in nine innings that season, despite having a career average of around 15. He played for the county for over twenty years, but missed six seasons through living in London.

As early as 1896 Mallett received a presentation for services to Durham County. By 1923 the county had made him Hon. Life Vice-President.

'Such services as these must almost create a record for cricket, and with them is coupled a gentleness and charm of manner; there is no wonder that he has attained the position he holds,' wrote Hon. Secretary William Bell.

After being its first secretary in the 1890s, Mallett was Chairman of the Minor Counties Cricket Association from 1909-31, and the first president elected in 1931. Sir Pelham Warner succeeded him.

In 1926 Mallett's cricket administration career took a twist when the MCC offered the services of its experienced committeeman to help set up the West Indies Cricket Board of Control ahead of its entry into test cricket in 1928.

Mallett advised on the formation of the new organisation and attended its inaugural meeting. He managed the West Indies on its 1928 tour to England, in which the Karl Nunes led team lost all three tests by an innings, with Jack Hobbs scoring his last test century in the second at The Oval.

This led to Durham's greatest administrator managing the 1929 MCC team to the West Indies and the 1930 West Indies team to Australia.

100
GREATS

Richard Anthony David Mercer
RHB & WK, 1975-88

Over fifteen stone and six feet tall, Richard Mercer had a background as striking as his appearance.

Brian Lander said broad cockney Mercer was 'one of the biggest characters, in every sense, that I ever played with'.

Mercer was born in Stockholm where his father worked. He later played for Young Middlesex XI and attended Durham University. He never left the area, meeting his future wife at University and becoming an administrator at Tynedale District Council in Hexham.

The surprisingly agile Mercer succeeded Tom Harland (who had replaced Bobby Cole) as Durham keeper when still at University, which was

unusual. Andy Fothergill came next, as part of a strong line of keepers. Both Harland and Mercer (as a batsman) played in the three wicket Gillette Cup loss to Northants in 1977.

Bigger than burly, the Durham City player was a key part of the Championship-winning sides of 1976, 1980, 1981 and 1984.

Though he never scored the runs he might have, batting unselfishly down the order, in 1981 his 50* helped Ashok Patel add 94 for the seventh wicket to hold off Norfolk in the end of season challenge at Durham City.

In 1983 Fothergill deputised for the injured Mercer, but the ageing keeper held onto the gloves until 1988. By then he had passed Cole's Durham dismissals record of 237 and his catches record of 165. He also ended up in the top ten Durham appearance makers, along with contemporaries Neil Riddell, Stephen Greensword and Steve Atkinson, with 126.

Lance Cairns was awestruck by the size of some of the local wicketkeepers: 'Alan Edgar at Bishops was 6ft 2ins and 23st, Mercer was 6ft and 18st; they were big boys to envisage as keepers, being that size and being able to move, but they did. Merce never had a bad game behind the stumps, and though there might have been better keepers around in the territory he was at the right club (Durham City) with Brian Lander. There was no problem with him being good enough to be in the side and every now

Richard Anthony David Mercer
Born: Stockholm, 14 January 1951
Died: Hexham, 25 October 1996
Also played for: Minor Counties

Batting

M	I	NO	Runs	
126	118	41	1,349	
Ave	100	50	Ct	St
17.51	0	4	183	66

and then he could and did score some runs. His keeping wasn't flashy, but he could stand up to me and not make mistakes.'

Mercer died of cancer aged 45 in 1996.

Colin Milburn

RHB & RM, 1959-76

Colin Milburn
Born: Burnopfield, 23 October 1941
Died: Aycliffe Village, 28 February 1990
Also played for: Northamptonshire, Western Australia, England

Batting

M	I	NO	Runs
3	4	0	101
Ave	100	50	Ct
33.50	1	0	1

More than anyone, 'Ollie' Milburn put Durham cricket on the map. Heroic, legendary, yet tragic, Milburn was the first former Durham player to make an impact at test level.

He was the North-East's George Best; a working-class lad made good thanks to his attacking, straightforward, entertaining opening batting.

Milburn's downfall, like Best's, was drink. Milburn went from test century-maker to near blindness inside a few weeks in 1969. His experience, a car crash in which he lost an eye, would have killed a poorer man. 'I have never been bitter about the accident,' he said, much later.

Son of a Burnopfield electrician and league cricketer, Milburn was the first of the post-National Service generation. He still took a traditional route out of the pit village: sport. Burnopfield's Jim McConnon, who played for England in 1954, had gone to Glamorgan via Aston Villa FC in 1950.

His Durham career rests on a single performance, against India in September 1959. Aged seventeen years and 324 days, the hefty right-handed opener won a standing ovation for whacking the Indian spinners for 101: 'An innings that gave me more personal delight than any before and many since.'

He had the choice of Warwickshire or Northants. Northants secretary Ken Turner offered one shilling a week more and Milburn became another recruit for scout Bill Coverdale. He developed steadily, but always remained the simple north easterner. Milburn won the Walter Lawrence Trophy for the fastest first-class century of both

1966 and 1967. He became a national hero. People could identify with his simple method and humble background and were entertained by his hitting.

He scored 94 on his test debut, hooking Wes Hall for six, against the West Indies in 1966 after being run out for nought in the first innings. In his second Test, at Lord's, Milburn hit 126*, with three sixes and 17 fours.

A Wisden Cricketer of the Year for 1967, he was both 'a scientific hitter and a character.'

He didn't pass fifty for two years and eight more Test innings, until, again at Lord's he made 83 against Australia in 1968. At The Oval Milburn, a surprisingly lithe short leg, caught 'corpse with pads' Bill Lawry. 'If they could have thrown Milburn aloft they would have,' wrote journalist Ian Wooldridge.

Called up from Western Australia as a replacement for the 1968/69 Pakistan tour, Milburn made 139 at Karachi. Like New Zealand's Gordon Leggat, selectors, against public and media opinion, deemed Milburn unsuitable for regular selection, probably due to fitness. And like Leggat, he proved them wrong when filling in for injured colleagues. Milburn never played properly again.

He returned to play for Northants and Durham in the mid-seventies without success. Malcolm Scott said: 'I knew a little of what fame did having played with Jackie Milburn. He had tremendous eyes for picking up the length ball. What an average player would hit for one or two he would hit for four or six.'

Milburn began a short commentary career, then returned to Durham to the pubs and clubs of his youth. He played for the Lord's Taverners until 1984. Milburn died of a heart attack in the pub car park of old mate Alan Edgar in 1990, aged 48.

---

100 GREATS

Alfred Morris
RHB & RM, 1905-14

Alfred Morris
Born: West Hartlepool, 11 September 1876
Died: Lancaster Moor, 29 March 1961
Also played for: Minor Counties

Batting

M	I	NO	Runs
94	143	36	1,133
Ave	100	50	
10.58	0	3	

Bowling

O	Md	R	W
3,125.3	694	8,459	651
Ave	5wI	10wM	Ct
12.99	67	26	49

Best Performance
10/130 v. Yorkshire II (at Barnsley), 1910

'The best bowler Durham ever had,' said Durham Hon. Secretary William Bell in his 1932 Golden Jubilee celebration of Durham CCC. 'Certainly the finest bowler ever to play for Durham County,' reiterated Brian Hunt half a century on in *100 Years of Durham County Cricket Club*.

A shipyard clerk who played in glasses, Morris' record is second to none for Durham, all achieved without much fuss, with a modest run up, an easy and a swinging medium-paced delivery batsmen. Morris used his powerful shoulders to combine body into arm action, producing a ball that nipped back from the off. The burly swing bowler also moved it away.

Next to the Minor Counties' finest, Sydney Barnes, Alf Morris was the most successful bowler in the competition's first half-century.

The only Durham player to take all ten, Morris received the inscribed match ball after the feat against Yorkshire II in 1910.

In 1911 he took more wickets than all of Durham's other bowlers added together. He only missed 100 by being unable to play in the Northumberland derby. Barnes outshone Morris' 97 at 10.98 with his 104 for Staffordshire.

Morris' total included 6/87 off 36 overs against All India, when he also scored 34* and 16 in the eight-wicket loss. Against the 1912 Australians he had similar figures of 6/96 off 32.2 overs, bowling Charlie Kelleway, Charlie Macartney, Warren Bardsley, David Smith, captain Claude Jennings and Gerry Hazlitt.

At a higher level he took 4/50 and 3/25 for an England XI against the 1912 Australians at Norwich and 3/5 before the rain came for Minor Counties against the South Africans in the same year.

Morris made his Durham debut aged eighteen when professional at Burnmoor. He was an outstanding performer from the start. He took 65 wickets at 13.16 in 1906, all after a bad start. Durham came fifth in the table and was third in the northern section the next year when he took 64 wickets at 12.40 in 298.5 overs.

Moving on to Sunderland as professional, where he was Edgar Elliot's team mate for a single season in 1907, Morris performed irresistibly for club and county, taking 731 wickets in seven seasons for Sunderland at an average of 7.15.

Always keen to bowl, he took 86 wickets at 12.24 in 428.5 overs in 1908, when Durham won six and lost one. He helped beat 1906, 1908 and 1911 champions Staffordshire with 14/67 in the match off 39.1 overs, surpassing Barnes' 4/65. At Ashbrooke, Morris dismissed seven of the last eight Staffordshire batsmen in the second innings to bring about a 10-wicket win. That season Morris (53*) set a tenth-wicket record with Jas Bewick (58), of 110 against Northumberland at Jesmond.

Combining effectively with 35-year-old leg spinner George Turnbull, Morris helped Durham to second in the Championship, despite a better win/loss ratio than Staffordshire. Perhaps Morris' best effort was bowling unchanged throughout both Lancashire II's innings at Blackpool, taking 7/50 and 6/28, then scoring a match-high 33 to secure victory.

While Morris' pace slowed to medium, his wicket taking speeded up. He bowled all seven in his 9/51, but missed out on the last wicket for his all-ten. Durham disappointed in 1909 and 1910, despite Morris' 122 wickets. He took 13/57 at King's Lynn against Norfolk, when he bowled unchanged again, but was overshadowed by Barnes' 12/91 (he took 2/70) in the loss to Staffordshire. He slipped in his all-ten, bowling seven, but tiring as Yorkshire II's Charlie Hardisty and Harry Hartington added 132 for the ninth wicket.

Now supported by Jim Thackeray, Morris, aged 34, found his peak form in 1911. Durham won seven out of ten, coming second to Staffordshire again. Morris was second to Barnes too, with 97 wickets to Barnes' 104. Barnes took 17/83 and scored 136 at South Shields, Morris just 6/123 in a season when he averaged 10.98 and struck on average every four overs. He took 10/154 at Stoke in the return, when Staffordshire was without Barnes, who was a current England player. Barnes took 189 test wickets – suggesting Morris' only slightly inferior figures (at least when Barnes wasn't there) meant he was good enough to be a first-class bowler. It never happened, as he preferred to stay in the leagues where he left Sunderland for Hendon in 1914 for an extra 5/- a week to take his wages to £4 a week.

Morris did not ease off Minor County batsmen, taking more than anyone did, with 87 wickets in 1913 and 65 in 1914, now helped by former Lancashire medium pacer Frank Harry.

His 651 wickets for Durham were 184 more than the next, Turnbull, when war ended cricket after 1914. Morris ended his Durham career with 9/36 including a hat trick against Cheshire.

After the war Morris, played into his fifties in the Bradford Leagues for Undercliffe, Low Moor, Bradford, Pudsey St Lawrence, Windhill and lastly in 1929, East Bierley.

John Edward Morris
RHB & RM, 1994-99

Johnny 'Animal' Morris had a brilliant county career, but was a fool to himself in that he wasted his talent. A flying prank ended his England hopes, and a move to Durham aged thirty did not revive them, though he set both run scoring and century records for the infant first-class county in six tempestuous seasons from 1994.

After trials with Warwickshire and Lancashire, coach Phil Russell recommended the Cheshire Schoolboys cricketer to Derbyshire in 1980.

In the eleven seasons following his debut in 1982, Morris scored prolifically at county level, with a best season of 1,739 runs in 1986. In 1990 he finally made the England team, and toured Australia that winter. He made his name by flying a biplane over a game he was playing in with David Gower and never played for England again.

The Mark Waugh-like Morris played in a Derbyshire team who won the Benson and Hedges Cup and the Sunday League, but needed a new challenge with no England call-up likely. He secured his release to play for Durham ahead of other counties keen to have him.

In 1994 he topped the averages with 1,369 Championship runs at 45.63 and in 1995 he made 1,297 first-class runs at 38.14 with three centuries.

He disappointed in 1996, but in 1997 returned close to his best form with 972 runs at 36.00 and

John Edward Morris			
Born: Crewe, 1 April 1964			
Also played for: Derbyshire, Griqualand West, Nottinghamshire, England			

Batting

M	I	NO	Runs
100	179	6	5,670
Ave	100	50	
32.77	14	23	

Bowling

O	Md	R	W
29.5	3	136	1
Ave	Ct		
136.00	45		

Best Performance
204 v. Warwickshire (at Birmingham), 1994

1,010 in all games, but in 1998 only 163 in the draw with Glamorgan showing what Wisden said was a 'glimpse of former glory' – in other words he had his right head on. Morris passed Larkins' record 10 centuries for Durham, but gave a two-fingered salute towards the Chester-le-Street crowd, who had barracked on passing the landmark and the club took 'appropriate disciplinary action' (Wisden) for the offensive gesture.

He handed over the vice-captaincy to Nick Speak for 1999, his benefit year, Durham's first for a player. Morris scored 792 runs at 31.68 with a period of 'mid season majesty' (Wisden) including 100 before lunch against Somerset after starting the second day on three. He reached 100 with a ball to spare, but hit the last delivery before the break straight to long leg. He passed 20,000 runs with 119 against Derbyshire, bringing up his 49th century with a second fifty in 31 balls of 'peerless strokes.' His form faded after Durham announced his release.

Tim Wellock summed up the feeling: 'There were few tears from the members; Morris had been perceived as expecting his huge talent to get him by, and gave the impression that, to bring out his best, he needed the motivation of top class bowling or his old Derbyshire colleagues. It was perfectly predictable his form would fade once it became clear he would not be retained.'

Always lacking restraint and keen on the big shot, Morris ended his career still occasionally showing his prodigious talent during two seasons at Nottinghamshire. He later became a sports agent.

100
GREATS

Maurice Nichol
RHB, 1923-26

Perhaps the most successful cricketer to have played for Durham before his early death in 1934, Maurice Nichol was on the fringe of the England team in the early 1930s.

The Eppleton club No.3, who began with Durham at the age of eighteen, top-scored for the county with 477 runs at 34.07 in the Championship-winning year of 1926. He then hit 496 at 29.33 in 1927. Keen to escape his mining background, after a trial at Surrey he moved to Worcestershire for 1928, scoring a century against the West Indies in his first first-class match.

Nichol was a success at Worcestershire, scoring 1,000 runs in a season four times, including 2,154 at 43.95 in 1933. His top score was 262* against Hampshire in 1930, then the second highest score for the county. Nichol was twelfth man for England against New Zealand in 1931, the season he represented Gentlemen v. Players.

However, he was always a sickly character. In the winter of 1931/32, he lay dangerously ill with pneumonia in Sunderland Royal Infirmary.

Nichol had a heart attack at Stratford Station on the way to Leytonstone to play Essex in 1933. By a tragic coincidence, the continuous strain of first-class cricket caught up again and he never woke up after retiring to bed after some light-hearted wrestling and smoking a pipe after the first day of the corresponding fixture a year later.

Nichol's path to top cricket began through Durham's foresight when the county employed former Surrey and Wearmouth professional Harry Clode and three others to coach youngsters to replace players lost in the war. The scheme produced first-class players Nichol and Leslie Wright (Worcestershire 1925-33) and Nichol's Eppleton team mate Harry Gibbon. Durham won the championship in 1926 and 1930 and the scheme's cost, £1,600 by 1931, looked money well spent.

Nichol scored two important centuries in 1926, and scored another against Lancashire II in 1927. In that year's match against New Zealand, he scored 19 and 56 in the ten wicket loss to New Zealand, when the freak 195 ninth wicket stand between Bertie Brooks and Jack Cook rescued Durham from an even bigger defeat.

Nichol's brother Ralph, a miner, was a slow left armer and left-handed bat who played for Bishop Auckland (professional 1931-33) and Durham (1924-27). Ralph, who scored a century, took a hat

Maurice Nichol			
Born: Hetton, 10 September 1904			
Died: Chelmsford, 21 May 1934			
Also played for: Worcestershire			

Batting

M	I	NO	Runs
51	78	3	2,016
Ave	100	50	
26.88	4	9	

Bowling

O	Md	R	W
10.1	1	58	3
Ave	Ct		
19.66	24		

Best Performance
130 v. H.D.G. Leveson-Gower XI, 1925

trick (against Normanby Hall) and saw his wife give birth on the same day in 1937. Ralph died in 1976.

Alan Gerald Bernard Old ———————— 100

RHB & RFM, 1968-78

Better known as a rugby international and brother of England cricketer Chris, all-rounder Alan Old was an important part of Durham's rise in the 1970s. From the Middlesbrough club, though he later played where rugby took him, (he played fly half for Middlesbrough, Leicester and Sheffield) to Worksop, Doncaster and Sheffield, Old won 16 rugby caps for England from 1972-78. He was on the winning team in just four games, although they were against Australia, South Africa, the All Blacks (16-10 at Auckland in 1973) and Wales.

Old was at his cricket peak in 1969, when the county was 19th, topping the averages with 230 runs at 46.00 and taking 12 wickets at 21.85 to win his county cap and the Player of the Year award. He played once for Warwickshire too; Chris followed him there from 1983-85.

He captained Durham occasionally in 1971 and 1972 between Bailey and Lander's tenures. Old took 1/33 in the first GC win, in 1972 against Oxfordshire and hit 39 in the next round loss to Surrey. Old opened the bowling economically against his home county Yorkshire in the 1973 landmark win, recording 0/10 off seven overs. Chris took 0/15 off eight for Yorkshire. Alan scored six and Chris, five. He was Durham's best player against

Alan Gerald Bernard Old			
Born: Middlesbrough, 23 September 1945			
Also played for: Warwickshire, Minor Counties			

Batting

M	I	NO	Runs
34	57	14	1,012
Ave	100	50	
23.53	0	2	

Bowling

O	Md	R	W
798.5	219	1,963	95
Ave	5wI	10wM	Ct
20.66	5	0	32

Best Performances
82* v. Staffordshire, 1972
6/20 v. Cumberland, 1969

Essex in 1973, his last GC match as rugby took over.

Uniquely, the Lions player once played for the England rugby team when Chris was playing for England at cricket. He is now principal of Redcar and Cleveland College (previously Sir William Turner's Grammar School).

David O'Sullivan

Born: Palmerston, New Zealand,
16 November 1944
Also played for: Central Districts, New Zealand,
Hampshire

Batting

M	I	NO	Runs
44	47	10	699
Ave	100	50	
18.99	1	1	

Bowling

O	Md	R	W
1,287.5	472	2,737	174
Ave	5wI	10wM	Ct
15.72	11	2	19

Best Performances
122* v. Northumberland, 1975
7/55 v. Staffordshire, 1976

Paid internationals, beginning with New Zealander David O'Sullivan, prompted Durham's most successful era in the late 1970s and 1980s.

A sharp turner of the ball who used flight skilfully, O'Sullivan played Hawke Cup cricket for Manawatu from 1962-69, with his first-class ambitions blocked by internationals Bryan Yuile and Vic Pollard.

Missing out on selection for the 1969 tour to England prompted O'Sullivan to move to Hampshire where, after qualifying (when he stayed in England working in removals), he played from 1971-73. He took 5/116 and 3/27 against India on his first-class debut and returned 29 wickets in 11 Championship matches in 1972 and 47 at 20.59 in 1973, bowling several sides out on late season worn pitches to help Hampshire to the title.

However, West Indies fast bowler Andy Roberts displaced him as overseas player for 1974. Roberts, who joined Barry Richards as Hampshire's overseas pair was yet to play a test. He was a revelation and the leading bowler of 1974, with 119 wickets at 13.62. 'Sully,' played for Central Districts from 1972/73, immediately winning selection to tour Australia with New Zealand's Coca-Cola knockout team. The next month he made his test debut against Pakistan.

After Hampshire, he turned down offers from Sussex and the Lancashire League, choosing Horden, a place he knew nothing about, in the DSCL. He said: 'I wanted a change. I didn't really like county cricket that much. League cricket wasn't as intense and we weren't playing every single day.'

He topped the Durham averages in his first season with 38 wickets at 13.86. Eppleton offered O'Sullivan better terms for 1974 and he left one cash-strapped colliery club for another, 'with no grudges at me going'.

O'Sullivan concurred with fellow Kiwi Lance Cairns in that 'most selections came from so-called fashionable clubs – Durham, Sunderland and Chester-le-Street to a certain extent. The colliery clubs didn't really get a look in.'

When O'Sullivan arrived at Eppleton with new wife Sandra in spring 1975 it snowed. O'Sullivan joined the World Cup squad, and a lonely Sandra moved in with club secretary Mr Thompson. Generosity like this meant O'Sullivan 'thoroughly enjoyed my time up there'.

Captain Brian Lander said O'Sullivan was a super bowler with a peculiar action. He was called for throwing by one-armed umpire Tom Drinkwater (O'Sullivan – 'a silly old fool: he was just a grumpy fellow who liked to stamp his authority. He felt hard done by probably because of his arm') in 1974 and remained under suspicion. O'Sullivan said: 'It didn't affect me at all.' His century against Northumberland in 1975 ('there was always a bit of tension in those games') was his fondest playing memory, though his performances when teaming up with Mohinder Armanath to form a formidable overseas duo in the 1976 Minor Counties title-winning team were his greatest contribution for Durham.

In 1976, his 8/78 in the match helped beat Cumberland at Ashbrooke and innings figures of 4/24 and 5/42 in the two wins over Oxfordshire took Durham towards the title. He was part of two title-winning teams that season, with his club Eppleton taking the DSCL from five-times-in-a-row champions Philadelphia.

He played in seven of his 11 tests while at Durham. After 1977 he stayed in New Zealand, ('I'd had enough of it – I couldn't see a future') retiring from Tests and running a sports shop in Napier, then going into insurance.

Norman William Owen
RHB & OB/RMF, 1947-55

Denied a place in the strong Surrey first eleven, Norman Owen came north after the war, playing as professional at Wearmouth and Sunderland before joining Bishop Auckland in 1951. He took over 80 wickets (best 102 in 1953) for Bishops each season from 1951-55, before moving on to Horden. He later returned to Bishops, for whom he took 435 wickets and scored 1,583 runs in all.

For Durham he took 6/49 on debut against Yorkshire II in 1947, followed by five wickets in each innings (10/81 in all) in a four wicket win over Lancashire II, with 29 at 16.58 in the season.

In 1949, his varied off spin yielded 41 wickets, his best in a season for Durham. Shortish and gaunt, he formed one of the county's best spin partnerships with leg spinner Bill Laidlaw, who took 58 wickets, also his season's best. However, the county, under Bill Proud, finished a lowly 16th in the table, and badly missed young players such as Dick Spooner, Alan Townsend and Stan Robertson, who had been snapped up by first-class counties.

Owen, Laidlaw (from Scotland) and Yorkshire's Ron Aspinall and Alec Coxon came in return, so perhaps the retirements of stalwarts David Townsend, Arnie Close and Freddie Herbert were a more significant factor, along with the strength of the first-class county's second elevens, in Durham's lack of success.

Owen's performances at a higher level hinted he could perhaps have been a successful first-class cricketer. In 1951, when Durham finished fourth, after a long run of Championship failure, Owen, a

Norman William Owen			
Born: London, 16 March 1915			
Died: Newton Aycliffe, 9 September 1977			
Also played for: Minor Counties, Surrey II			
Batting			
M	I	NO	Runs
67	83	12	1,057
Ave	100	50	
14.88	0	1	
Bowling			
O	Md	R	W
1,441.4	350	3,647	185
Ave	5wI	10wM	Ct
19.71	16	1	44
Best Performances			
88* v. Yorkshire II, 1948			
7/16 v. Lancashire II, 1949			

local authority worker, played for Minor Counties v. Kent taking 1/33 and scoring 14 and 12. The slim Londoner also played four times for Durham against touring teams, a highlight bowling Clyde Walcott for 67 in 1950 at Ashbrooke.

An excellent, enthusiastic coach at Bishop Auckland right up to his death, he bowled spin for most of the latter part of his career. To Durham's benefit, even if he'd stayed at Surrey where Alec Bedser stood in front of him as a seamer, Jim Laker and Tony Lock would have kept him out as a spinner.

Cecil Harry Parkin
RHB & LB/OB, 1907-13

'The story goes that the first noise I made in my cradle sounded like 'How's that?' wrote Ciss Parkin. But being born in Durham made his a convoluted road to cricket success.

Parkin's birthplace, twenty yards from the Yorkshire border, blighted his early ambitions. After a single game for Yorkshire, when Lincolnshire-born captain Lord Hawke decided to

Cecil Harry Parkin
Born: Egglescliffe, 18 February 1886
Died: Manchester, 15 June 1943
Also played for: Yorkshire, Lancashire, England

Batting

M	I	NO	Runs
16	23	3	231
Ave	100	50	
11.55	0	0	

Bowling

O	Md	R	W
239	44	731	56
Ave	5wI	10wM	Ct
13.05	4	2	3

Best Performance
6/37 v. Lincolnshire, 1912

overlook Parkin's lack of a birth qualification, someone (Parkin didn't know who) told the authorities and the 20-year-old off spinner waited eight seasons for his career to restart. In the meantime he played for Durham, but pointedly hardly alluded to the time in any of his three books. He preferred to justify, speculate and make jokes, rather like in the modern cricket autobiography. But in the 1920s this meant trouble, and Parkin's newspaper column criticisms of England captain Arthur Gilligan cost him his England career in 1924.

For England, Parkin could have been great, but he played against a dominating Australian team in nine of his 10 Tests. He debuted with Patsy Hendren, C.A.G. 'Jack' Russell and Abe Waddington in 1920/21, taking 1-58 and 3-102. England lost by 377 runs. Lean and of medium height, Parkin, the first former Durham player to play Tests, (and, after Drewy Stoddart, the second Durham-born test player) played in losing teams in his first seven Tests. He took 24 wickets, but never appeared on a winning team until 1924, when Arthur Gilligan and Maurice Tate bowled South Africa out for 30 at Edgbaston.

For Durham, Parkin never played the tourists and only made 16 appearances in seven seasons. A former apprentice pattern maker, Parkin had higher aspirations than Minor County cricket. He played for Norton-on-Tees first XI aged ten, firstly as a batsman in the NYSD League. The Whitwells, Nigel Harrison (London County, MCC, Durham 1902 and 1905) and William Hemingway (Gloucestershire) were in the team. He improved his bowling in the Staffordshire League with Tunstall, becoming a master of variation of pace and spin. From 1910 he played for Church and was leading wicket taker for the club each year until 1915.

Parkin's best performances for Durham, for whom he played in 1907, 1909, 1912 and 1913, came in his last two seasons as a Minor County player.

In 1912 he took 31 wickets at 12.51 in six games, partnering Morris, who took 49 at 14.02, as Durham finished a disappointing sixth. He took 10-74 (6-37 and 4-37) in tandem with Morris (7-65) against Lincolnshire in 1912 and 10-108 (Morris 10-100) against Northumberland (who were bowled out twice in 59 overs) the following season, his last before his Lancashire debut in 1914. He took 6-39 in his only other 1913 appearance against Staffordshire, but was overshadowed by the Minor Counties' greatest product Sydney Barnes. Parkin was perhaps the second best produced by the new competition pre-First World War, but Barnes demonstrated his pre-eminence by taking 6/31 and 4/12, and scoring 54 and 55* as Staffs won by 166 runs. Parkin moved onto Lancashire for 1913, Barnes having left the county for Staffs a decade earlier.

Parkin is best remembered for his humour; he used to conjure the ball out of his pocket, or flick it from his toe onto his head. The Clown Prince of Cricket's humour is now dated, but his run-ins with Lord's authority have a timeless quality.

Alan Herring Parnaby

RHB & RM, 1936-39

Alan Herring Parnaby
Born: Sunderland, 2 September 1916
Died: London, 25 November 1974
Also played for: Minor Counties,
 Combined Services

Batting

M	I	NO	Runs
30	53	4	1,279
Ave	100	50	
26.10	2	4	

Bowling

O	Md	R	W
81	5	384	13
Ave	5wI	10wM	Ct
29.53	1	0	6

Best Performances
162 *v.* Northumberland, 1939
5/39 *v.* Staffordshire, 1937

Durham's leading Army cricketer Alan Parnaby eschewed a possible first-class career to serve the country. The best Sunderland batsman since Edgar Elliot, Parnaby began his senior cricket as a schoolboy in 1932. He scored 4,554 runs at 45.00 in seven seasons for Sunderland, with eight centuries.

The attractive right-handed opener made his Durham debut at the same time as Arnie Close, Arthur Austin and Tom Taylor, against Northumberland, in 1936. That year he added 109 for the first wicket with Ned Randle (85) in the second innings, setting Durham up for a five wicket win against India.

He had an outstanding game *v.* Staffordshire at South Shields in 1937, scoring 90* and taking 5/39 as the seventh bowler David Townsend used, having future England batsman (1946-55) Jack Ikin caught for 123. Parnaby, who rarely bowled, said: 'I'll have to see that in print before I believe it.'

In 1937 the tall and strong batsman scored 14 and 18 against New Zealand. Opposing opener Walter Hadlee said: 'I think I got him out. He was probably my only wicket on tour! But he was a very good player.'

Having hit 118* against Lancashire II in 1938, Parnaby scored 162 against Northumberland in 1939, when he shared the Durham captaincy with Austin and Randle when Townsend was absent

and also played for Minor Counties, for whom he scored a century on debut, against Oxford University. But his Durham days were over and he subsequently played his cricket for the Army and Combined Services (1949-53).

Parnaby then joined the Army in 1939, captained Army and Services sides and won promotion to become Aide-de-Camp to the Queen and a Brigadier. After the war he led the British Army of the Rhine side and other services sides as well as the MCC.

D.G. Greig said of Parnaby in *The History of Sunderland* CC: 'Admirable in spirit and competence alike, once he has settled down he seemed incapable of a bad stroke. He treated the good ball cautiously, the indifferent he hit hard with a lovely range of scoring strokes. Had his lot been cast with a first-class county he would certainly have made his mark.'

Ashok Sitaram Patel

LHB & SLA, 1981-91

One of the first of the wave of Durham University players of the 1980s and 1990s, Ash Patel settled in the North and brought much to league and county cricket in Durham.

A versatile hard hitter, who could have been playing county cricket, Patel was the ideal type of player for Durham's successful team.

Three failed county players starred in Durham's glory years of the 1980s. Two were veteran all-rounders Steve Greensword and Peter Kippax. The other was Patel, who had played with England captains Mike Brearley, Mike Gatting and John Emburey, but been denied a place by England slow left armer Phil Edmonds.

Ashok Sitaram Patel
Born: Nairobi, Kenya, 23 September 1956
Also played for: Middlesex

Batting

M	I	NO	Runs
109	161	37	4,120
Ave	100	50	
33.22	3	22	

Bowling

O	Md	R	W
947.5	207	3,168	114
Ave	5wl	10wM	Ct
27.78	2	0	63

Best Performances
108* v. Cumberland, 1982
5/80 v. Lincolnshire, 1991

Patel played just two matches in 1978 and returned north after not being re-engaged.

He said: 'It was a rough time in London. There were no two-year contracts forthcoming so I came back to Durham where I had met my wife while at university. I didn't think it was a much different standard in the Minor Counties, except we were all working and couldn't practice every day like they do.'

At Burnmoor from 1981-83 and Hetton Lyons in 1984-85, Patel was still an excellent league professional at Philadelphia in his mid forties, then at South Shields, where ex-Durham player Peter Crane recruited him, from 2001. Patel started stunningly with Durham scoring 89 in the 1981 challenge match, seventh wicket 94 with Mercer against Norfolk at Durham City. He slammed 498 runs in the 1984 Championship winning campaign.

Patel's all-round play matured through the 1980s ('It was down to experience, you had to take your chance when it came') and he topped the 1991 averages at over 50 with the bat and 25 wickets at under 15 to win the Frank Edwards Trophy. In his last game his lightly spun off spin brought a career best 5/80 to force a win over Lincolnshire, who had been set 244 in 132 minutes plus 20 overs by a Neil Riddell declaration.

Patel became a geography and PE teacher at Shotton Hall Comprehensive School on his return from London, and has stayed there ever since.

100
GREATS

Joseph Albert Pease
RHB & WK, 1882-92

Half a century of Parliamentary service somewhat overshadows the cricket career of Jack Pease, created Lord Gainford, first Baron of Headlam Hall in 1917.

Educated to MA level at Trinity College Cambridge University, he was master of the draghounds, a polo player and cricket team twelfth man. Pease's Quaker family had made and lost a fortune in railways, mining, iron foundries and banking in the nineteenth century.

Durham's second captain after Alf Mewburn, Pease played for Darlington and was regular wicket-keeper, as well as an occasional lob bowler. He also played for the MCC before his retirement aged 32.

In 1902, Barclay's Bank found the Pease family bankrupt, after a university chum of Jack's married his heiress sister Beatrice, the Countess of Plymouth, who then won half a million pounds compensation from their father Sir Joseph for his dishonest mismanagement of her inheritance.

Jack rebuilt the family reputation. He was Durham captain from 1886-91, the country's youngest Mayor at Darlington in 1889, and only stopped playing cricket for Durham when elected Liberal MP for Tyneside in 1892. He served as MP for Saffron Waldon (1901-10) and Rotherham (1910-16) before elevation to the Lords.

The modest, frank, courteous, loyal Parliamentarian entered the cabinet in 1910 as Chancellor of the Duchy of Lancaster and was an influential President of the Board of Education from 1911-15 and Postmaster-General in 1916. Despite his industrial and scientific background as chairman of the Durham Coal Owners Association and National and Durham Coke Owners, the Government gave the disinterested Gainford the job of Chairman of the BBC from 1922-26 and Vice Chairman from 1926-32.

He was president of the Confederation of British Industries in 1927-28 and remained a leading advocate for the coal industry until his death.

Joseph Albert Pease
Born: Darlington, 17 January 1860
Died: Headlam Hall, 15 February 1943

Batting

M	I	NO	Runs
29	49	10	745
Ave	100	50	
19.10	0	2	

Bowling

O	Md	R	W
1	0	8	0
Ct	St		
22	4		

Best Performance
89 v. Yorkshire Gentlemen, 1884

Andrew Pratt
LHB & WK, 1998-date

Andrew Pratt
Born: Crook, 14 March 1975

Batting

M	I	NO	Runs	
48	80	11	1,356	
Ave	100	50	Ct	St
19.65	0	6	117	10

Best Performance
93 v. Gloucestershire, 2002

Durham's most talented wicketkeeper had to wait in line to succeed to the gloveman position after making his debut in friendly matches aged sixteen. Andrew Pratt did not establish himself until 2001 when he won his cap and displaced Martin Speight from the first team.

Pratt made his Durham II debut in 1994 and was an MCC Young Cricketer for three years, as was his elder brother Neil, who also represented the seconds. Father Gordon kept wicket for Durham City and younger brother Gary made his first-class debut for Durham in 2000. The boyish left-handed opener won the Batsman of the Year award two years later.

Andrew Pratt had won the Player of the Year award in 2001, his first full season behind the

stumps after three years in Speight's shadow. He had made his debut in 1998, scoring 34 out of 122 in the second innings before being dropped back to the seconds for more than a year. A good example of the nurturing system at Durham, the slim, youthful Pratt was the sole remaining pre-first-class player on the books by 2003.

A specialist keeper who recognised the need to contribute with the bat, Pratt argued top-class glovework should be worth a place without additional batting skills. Always keen to stand up, Pratt said his only coach was his father, other than a few tips from Alan Knott when he was at Lord's, after which he had almost gone to Leicestershire.

Choosing the right Pratt to watch could be difficult for the brothers' parents. 'The whole family are mad keen on the game and either my dad or my mum will be watching Gary or me. If we're in the same side it helps and it was a great day out when we became the first brothers to represent Durham.'

After 10 games in three years, Pratt's chance came when Speight ricked his neck in the first match of 2001 against Durham UCCE. Pratt took his opportunity so well he caught 71 and stumped 18 in all competitions in the season, inhibiting batsmen by standing up and winning the praise of the Durham faithful.

He opened the batting in one-dayers, playing the pinch hitter role and averaging 34. In the Championship his 476 runs came at 20, but promised more with his stylish hitting in years to come.

However, after being mentioned in newspapers as a possible replacement for England's Alec Stewart, Durham dropped him in favour of Phil Mustard, a better batsman.

Meanwhile, brother Gary scored his maiden century and established himself in the Durham top order in 2003, hitting more than 1,000 first-class runs, after beginning the season as much less of a certainty for a place than Andrew.

Ernest Barton Proud
RHB, 1906-19

Ernest Barton Proud
Born: Bishop Auckland, 6 December 1880
Died: Bishop Auckland, 15 June 1967

Batting

M	I	NO	Runs
43	70	6	1,037
Ave	100	50	Ct
16.20	1	3	11

Best Performance
103 v. Yorkshire II, 1908

Ernest Proud was the grand old man of Durham cricket when he died, six years after his son Bill, also a Durham captain, in 1967. They are the only father and son to captain the county.

Educated at Charterhouse, gentleman farmer Proud was a club cricketer for Bishop Auckland who made occasional appearances for the county.

Tall, steady, angular, quiet and correct, he scored his only century, and Durham's sole hundred of 1908 (the season after Edgar Elliot left), in a seventh wicket partnership of 178 with George Turnbull that took Durham from 111/6 to 356. Durham subsequently won the game against Yorkshire II by 136 runs. At the turn of the century Bishop Auckland FC player Proud won three amateur international football caps as a goalkeeper.

Proud replaced Charles Young Adamson, who had gone to Australia, as Durham CCC captain in 1913. He led the side in two full seasons, and relinquished the captaincy to Tom Kinch soon after the First World War ended.

In 1913 Durham won five out of 10, for fifth place in the table, but just one win off the title. Alf Morris took 87 wickets and Frank Harry 48, leaving Proud little to do except urge his batsmen to get the runs required. Morris took 65 wickets in 1914, with Harry collecting 44, but Durham finished 13th in 1914, although it won its final match before the war suspended the Championship for six seasons.

The solicitor and registrar for Bishop Auckland followed brewery giant William Nimmo as Durham chairman from 1937-63 and was Bishop Auckland president from 1940-67.

Roland Barton Proud
RHB & RM, 1946-55

Bill Proud was one of Durham's cricketing blue bloods. His grandfather, John Thomas Proud was Bishop Auckland coroner, and his father, Ernest, a county and club captain and administrator. Following his father as Bishop Auckland and Durham captain, Bill Proud was a hard-hitting attractive batsman, who favoured the straight drive.

He played for Winchester First XI from 1936-38. In 1938 he made 84 and 102 out of 136 in 49 minutes for The Rest v. Lord's Schools, then 96 and 34 for Public Schools the next day. The dashing middle order batsman played for Hampshire in 1938-39, then at Oxford University where he won a blue as a freshman in 1939, scoring 19 and 87 in the Varsity

Roland Barton Proud
Born: Bishop Auckland, 29 September 1919
Died: Bishop Auckland, 27 October 1961
Also played for: Hampshire, Oxford University

M	I	NO	Runs
74	101	3	2,309
Ave	100	50	Ct
23.56	3	9	24

Best Performance
112 v. Yorkshire II, 1950

match. The war intervened, and Proud then played for Durham, captaining the side from 1948-55. Durham was not in a successful period until his final years, finishing 16th, 16th, 22nd, 4th, 10th, 26th, 5th and 3rd.

As a batsman, he scored 319 runs in 1946, including 108 v. Lancashire II, before taking over from David Townsend, who had broken a wrist, during 1947. His last first-class match was for Minor Counties in 1950, when he made his career's best innings.

In 1953 he headed the averages with 336 runs at 30.54 and in 1954 he hit 110 v. Yorkshire II as Durham shot back up the Minor County table mainly thanks to performances from experienced players such as Jack Keeler, Harry Bell and Alec Coxon.

Proud could be authoritarian, as when he sacked the argumentative Alec Coxon, but the 'Durham Ox' had a weakness of his own. Before the 1955 season, thickset and ruddy Proud resigned the captaincy, the reason given being business and farming commitments. Don Hardy took over. Proud collected rents as a gentleman farmer, but never really worked and developed a drink problem which eventually killed him.

He scored 5,896 runs for Bishop Auckland after making his debut aged 14 in 1934. He captained for 11 seasons until his retirement in 1959 due to illness. He appeared once in 1961, but died that October aged 42. His brother Leslie also played for Bishop Auckland.

Neil Riddell

LHB & RM, 1972-90

Taking over from the gentlemanly Brian Lander as Durham captain in 1980, Neil Riddell was already 32 and well advanced towards county runscoring and appearance records. Lander's Durham had beaten Yorkshire in the GC, won the championship after a 46-year break and finished runners-up in 1977, 1978 and 1979. Yet Riddell's side did better still as he brought a new toughness to the team, with a win at all costs attitude.

'He did take the emphasis on playing hard cricket,' said Riddell's match winner Lance Cairns. 'He was no nonsense guy. Winning was the whole thing to him and that's why he played the game. He was a good leader, but bore the brunt of a few jokes from Paul Romaines and Steve Atkinson. Riddell tried to talk posh, but he wasn't.'

'Jimmy' Riddell said that Cairns helped in his early years as captain to set challenges and be an

Neil Riddell
Born: Staindrop, 16 July 1947
Also played for: Minor Counties

Batting

M	I	NO	Runs
218	313	61	8,694
Ave	100	50	Ct
34.50	6	53	111

Best Performance
139 v. Hertfordshire, 1980

attacking, positive captain. Cairns said 'Riddell was a guy who would always take the challenge maybe he needed somebody to give confidence.'

He led Durham to three Championships in his

arrogant if you want, but yes, I think we were, as we liked to play with a bit of swagger. However, in the end it's all about ability and team spirit and we never lacked both'.

With Atkinson and Steve Greensword, he had formed the heart of the Durham side since the first GC win, against Yorkshire in 1973, when he made 15 on his competition debut, leaving Durham just 15 to win.

His hard-hitting left hand batting brought success for both Durham and Minor Counties. He was twenty-eight when he hit his first Durham century, but ended with six and a record 53 half-centuries. In 1978 he scored a Durham record of 952 runs, which he followed by 508 in 1979, 597 in 1980 and 545 in 1981, showing his batting was unaffected by the captaincy, which he kept until the 1991 watershed.

Although he was captain when Durham ended its 65-match unbeaten streak in 1982 against Staffordshire at Stockton, he still went for the win, with Staffs getting home by two wickets. Riddell said of the record: 'Not once during this period did Durham play for a draw or play negatively to protect it.'

Riddell played for Lands, Raby Castle and Barnard Castle before longer stints at Bishop Auckland 66-76 and Darlington from 1977.

A huge gambler on the horses, Riddell was never frightened to lose, which translated itself to his cricket captaincy. Probably the best skipper Durham ever had, he stayed on the committee after Durham went first-class, but had reservations about the demise of the non-professional representative side. Often regarded as arrogant, Riddell was a non-conformist who was unpopular with opposing captains. His will to win didn't sit well with the Minor County pattern, but the Darlington roofers managing director left a legacy of success that ensured Durham first-class status.

first five seasons as captain, as well as the English Estates Trophy and a win against Derbyshire in the 1985 NWT. This came when his 49* took Durham to a seven wicket win, to make Durham the first Minor County to have beaten two first class sides.

Riddell said of the Derbyshire win: 'There were no great feelings of ecstasy about it – we just felt we were in charge and had done a good job. But Yorkshire was a different story in 1973, no side had done that before, so it was the first. That made it special. Over the years we went from strength to strength because we knew we were good. Call it

Wasim Hasan Raja

100 GREATS

LHB & RLB, 1978-87

Wasim Raja was something of a paradox. He was an attacking middle order batsman and an elaborate wrist spinner, who became an international cricket referee. The Pakistani also enjoyed the traditional northern activity of drinking pints.

Lance Cairns said: 'Waz was the dasher. He'd score 100 before lunch. He liked to get on with the job and backed himself to score runs quickly. He wasn't worried about reputations. When he did get

runs it was brilliant stuff to watch. He always wanted to win. When Kippax wasn't around he'd do the leg spin bowling. He loved a drink: a good man to cotton on with after a game. He was the exception to the rule. He took a shine to Christopher (Cairns) and would steal him for the weekend when he was nine or ten. He loved telling jokes.'

Wasim came into the Durham team in 1978 scoring 626 runs in 1979 in one the strongest

Durham line-ups. With Steve Atkinson, Neil Riddell, Paul Romaines, Steve Greensword, Lance Cairns, Peter Kippax and Stuart Wilkinson in the side, Durham was becoming an irresistible combination, except in the Gillette Cup against Yorkshire.

Wasim scored 52 in Durham's 213/9 in front of 5,000 at Ropery Lane, but Yorkshire won by four wickets thanks to Geoff Boycott's 92. It was a similar story in 1980, when Wasim's 53 and 2/50 (Clive Rice and Richard Hadlee) couldn't stop a four-wicket win by Nottinghamshire.

However, that season Durham won the Minor County Championship, with Wasim's 626 runs and performances such as 8.4-8-2-4 against Cumberland at Millom showed the difference to the county of an established international.

In 1981 Durham won the Championship again, with six-hit specialist Wasim scoring 662 runs. His highlight was 166 *v.* Norfolk, including 122 in boundaries in the challenge match at Durham City.

Bearded, slight and urbane, Wasim was professional at Chester-le-Street from 1978-80, Whitburn in 1981 and Durham City in 1982. He went to Northumberland in 1983, but returned to Shotley Bridge in 1984.

For Chester-le-Street he once took 95 wickets and scored 960 runs in season, coming closest to be first to do the double in the DSCL. In Pakistan, where his brothers Rameez and Zaeem were first-class players, in 1973/74 he'd scored 1,010 runs at 32.58 and taken 99 wickets at 22.41.

He toured England in 1974 (scoring 486 runs at 54.00) and in 1978, and played in the 1975 and 1979 World Cups. In 1979/80 he hit 450 runs at 56.25 *v.* India and 246 at 61.5 *v.* West Indies,

---

Wasim Hasan Raja
Born: Multan, Pakistan, 3 July 1952
Also played for: Lahore, Sargodha, Punjab University, Combined Universities, Pakistan International Bank, Northumberland, Pakistan

Batting

M	I	NO	Runs
48	71	10	2,428
Ave	100	50	
39.80	2	18	

Bowling

O	Md	R	W
589.1	164	1,702	67
Ave	5wI	10wM	Ct
25.40	3	0	25

Best Performances
166 *v.* Norfolk, 1981
5/40 *v.* Cheshire, 1981

---

showing he was at the peak of his form when at Durham.

In 1982 he toured England again, but was dropped after the first test. Without Wasim and Cairns, Durham dropped to ninth place in the Championship.

Wasim left to play for Northumberland in 1984, but returned to Durham for three games in 1987, scoring 71 runs in five innings and taking three wickets for 161. The explosive, uninhibited left handed bat who used a full follow through, was a popular and attractive cricketer in the North-East, combining well with the less refined abilities of Lance Cairns. He settled in the area marrying an English woman and coaching cricket.

Paul William Romaines ———————————— 100
RHB & OB, 1977-81

The most talented of Durham's batsmen in the glory days of the late 1970s, Paul Romaines had the ambition and luck to take his career further.

However, his planned return to his home team failed as, after being a prime mover for Durham's first-class status in 1992, Geoff Cook vetoed his inclusion in the squad and the Gloucestershire middle order batsman missed the playing role he yearned for.

Earlier Romaines had helped establish Lance Cairns at Bishop Auckland and had been the main

joker in the Durham side that finished either second or first in his five seasons with the county. Romaines was the link between Gloucestershire's David Graveney and Durham, but all he got in the end was a commercial manager job.

'He was the one player Geoff (Cook) and I had different views about,' Graveney said. 'Perhaps it was because I felt I was committed to Paul, having spoken to him about playing, or perhaps it was because I knew him better than most people, and always got the best out of him when I was captain during our time at Gloucestershire. He is a marvel-

Paul William Romaines
Born: Bishop Auckland, 25 December 1955
Also played for: Northamptonshire,
Gloucestershire, Griqualand West

Batting

M	I	NO	Runs
42	70	8	1,892
Ave	100	50	Ct
30.51	1	10	20

Best Performance
133 v. Suffolk, 1979

lous enthusiast, but Geoff said there was no room.'

Cook ruminated on players moving counties and Romaines 'unusual route' in Romaines' 1991 benefit brochure. Cook said Romaines deserved his reward most of all for his love of the game. But at the age of 36, Cook felt Romaines was an unnecessary addition to the Durham squad. Romaines' humour lapsed as he missed out on a 10-year old shared dream with Graveney. He did not go to players' get togethers and resigned from his job at Durham in February 1991 when the players were in Zimbabwe.

Romaines was an England school trialist with Graham Stevenson and Ian Botham in 1971. All three failed to make the team. He played for Bishop Auckland then Northamptonshire after Durham County Schoolboys coach Doug Ferguson scouted him in 1973. Ferguson also discovered Colin Milburn, Peter Willey, Cook and George Sharp.

Later Romaines played for Alnwick (1977/78 Northumberland League), Synthonia and Darlington (1980/81) scoring 1,880 runs at 49.47 in the NYSD.

Too happy-go-lucky for the coaches at Northamptonshire, Romaines returned north and in his 1977 Durham debut season he made 92* v. Staffordshire at Stockton, a match Durham won by 102 runs. The team was second in table after drawing the challenge match v. Suffolk. Durham was also runner up in 1978 and 1979, with Romaines scoring 650 runs in 1979, second best behind Steve Atkinson's 723.

Desperate to be a first-class player, he sent a circular to the counties in 1980 asking for a trial, though he had a job as a L'Oreal representative. 'I just felt that after four years of league cricket I was a much tighter batsman, so I took the gamble,' he said. He received four replies, one from Gloucestershire's Tony Brown.

In May 1981, he played v. Somerset II, got dropped off a hook on 17, made 128 and won a contract. He scored 186 v. Warwickshire 1982 to save the match after being under pressure for his place, when Graveney said if he didn't get some runs, he would be dropped. In a 1985 Sunday League match, Romaines, after an afternoon affected by rain, and Pimms, accidentally smashed Leicestershire's Ian Butcher's nose while perfectly executing a follow through in the dressing room.

Romaines, now a sports master at Clifton College, came from a cricketing family, with his grandfather Billy playing for Durham in 1925/26.

Lance Cairns said: 'Out of all the players in the top order Romaines was the one with the most ability and the best range of shots with a good enough brain to go quite a long way in the game. He wouldn't give his wicket away, he'd bat four or five hours, he kept the ball on the ground, didn't worry about lofting, and was equally at home against spin and pace. He was a very good cover fieldsman, quick to get the ball in. The sort of player people loved to have on side always up to something, if you had a bad day Paul wasn't the sort of character to sit around and mope about it, he'd do something stupid and he'd get the team going again.'

100
GREATS

Michael Anthony Roseberry
RHB & RM, 1995-98

Micky Roseberry rode into Durham in 1995 with the hopes of the whole county on his shoulders. He failed to bear the weight and returned to Middlesex for a benefit in 2000 after four seasons of failure.

The former Durham School pupil joined Middlesex in 1984 and went on to play 236 first-class and 204 limited over games in his career.

Roseberry's father Matt was a director of Durham CCC, who, with Mike Weston, sent their sons to Lord's for coaching and later opened his own Durham school in 1986. Phil and Robin Weston prospered outside Durham, as did Roseberry and his brother Andrew, who played for Leicestershire.

After attending Tonstall Preparatory School in Durham, Roseberry played as a professional in the

Michael Anthony Roseberry
Born: Sunderland, 28 November 1966
Also played for: Middlesex

Batting

M	I	NO	Runs
43	78	5	1,805
Ave	100	50	
24.72	1	9	

Bowling

O	Md	R	W	Ct
3.4	0	19	0	28

Best Performance
145* v. Oxford University, 1996

Durham Senior Cricket League while still at Durham School, where he had scored 216 in 160 minutes against St Bees aged 16. His school record of 3,813 runs at 63.55 from 1981-85 included 1,288 runs at an average of over 100 and captaincy of ESCA against MCC Schools in 1984 and a tour to the West Indies with England Young Cricketers in 1985. In 1984, the prodigy played for Durham in the Minor County title play-off against Cheshire, but he joined Middlesex for 1985.

As a right-handed opener, Roseberry formed an effective opening partnership with Desmond Haynes, who sometimes shielded him from the strike, helping Middlesex win the County Championship in 1990 and 1993, as well as the Sunday League in 1992. Roseberry admired Haynes, 'for the obvious' reasons.

His best year came in 1992, when he made 2,044 runs, was named Middlesex Player of the Year, was the country's joint leading run scorer and won a place on the England 'A' tour to Australia that winter. Roseberry's career was faltering when he was tempted by another false dawn at Durham, but he wasn't to know the move would be a mistake.

Roseberry, aged 34 when he retired, tellingly said: 'I've had a great time in first-class cricket and enjoyed every moment. I'd like to thank both Durham, but particularly Middlesex, the players and the members for their support over the years and for the many happy memories I have.'

Bulky and 6ft 1in, Roseberry scored 11,950 first-class runs at 33.37, as well as 5,674 at 30.83 in limited overs matches.

He won his Middlesex cap in 1990. In 1994 he averaged 36.56. In 1995, his first year at Durham he averaged 24.77, scoring 669 runs with a highest score of 90. He never made a Championship century for Durham, though he did score 145* against Oxford University in 1996, adding a Durham all wicket record of 334 unbroken with Stewart Hutton. He also hit 121 in the NWT against Herefordshire in 1995.

His captaincy and batting for Durham was a disaster against any top-class opposition. He scored 458 first-class runs at 16.96 in 1996, 69 in 1997 and 295 at 26.81 in 1998 in the County Championship, when he made three centuries, (the same as 1997) including a 238*, for the seconds.

He represented Durham county at age group rugby level and moved home to join his father's business empire on his retirement.

Malcolm Ernest Scott ———————————— 100
RHB & SLA, 1953-56   GREATS

Part of the 1950s drain to first-class counties. Northamptonshire did particularly well in Durham, with George Johnson, Henry Greenwood, William Barron (lesser-known players) preceding Colin Milburn, Scott, Gus Williamson, Peter Willey, George Sharp, Alan Tait, Alan Hodgson, Paul Romaines and Grant Forster, who all played at Northampton in the 1960s and 1970s.

Malcolm Ernest Scott
Born: South Shields, 8 May 1936
Also played for: Northamptonshire

Batting

M	I	NO	Runs
29	41	9	602
Ave	100	50	
18.81	0	3	

Bowling

O	Md	R	W
572.4	157	1,392	65
Ave	5wI	10wM	Ct
21.41	3	1	10

Best Performances
98* v. Northumberland, 1956
6/30 v. Staffordshire, 1955

South Shields spinner Scott said he was 'more of a batsman,' 'a young lad among these great fellas' when he took 14 wickets at 21.14 in debut season 1953 ('happy youthful days') as Durham finished fifth in Proud's last season as captain. He took 10/90 v. Staffordshire in 1955, the year he was hit for 111 off 22 overs by the South African tourists, who rattled up 543 in the innings and 324 run win at Ashbrooke. Scott took the wickets of Anton Murray and Russell Endean, and then batting at No.6, made nought and 16.

He said: 'The Durham days were magic. I was working in the shipyards and getting off to play. It deferred me from going to sea; it did me good.'

He did his National Service at the same time as Williamson from 1957, and then joined Williamson at Northants. Talented footballer Scott made his first-class debut for Combined Services in 1958 and progressed to take 113 wickets at 19.27 in 1964, forming a potent bowling/batting North-East duo with Milburn.

But it all went wrong for both players. Playing inland on the Northampton 'billiard table' affected his bowling and umpires reported Scott for a suspect action in 1967, and he was banned from county cricket.

Scott said: 'County cricket was a hard game especially as a bowler. You had to be absolutely top-notch. God knows why I went to Northants. They had no end of left arm spinners there. I asked for my release when I got there because we had a staff of twenty-six with a surfeit of good players. County cricket was very hard compared with league and Minor County cricket, playing six days a week and not going home after taking 5/28 at Wood Terrace. You're with each other all the time, which is wonderful if you get 150, but on the other side, it's terrible if you drive from Dover to Sheffield and take 0/20 and get a double duck; it's a psychological thing. If the skipper loses the toss against Padgett, Ken Taylor, Closey suddenly you think to yourself, "God, is there any rain about." If it's a game on Saturday you're dying to play; if it rains it's the most disappointing thing in the world. In County Cricket if it rains you're glad to put your feet up.'

At the age of 33, the Newcastle and Darlington FC half-back's career was over by the end of 1969, the same year Milburn lost an eye in a car crash. Tragedy for Scott and Milburn, but more North-East league cricketers were ready to take step in at Northants, which had weak leagues, with Sharp, Willey, Cook, Hodgson and Tait joining the staff between 1966-71. Scott went on to sell Newbury and Gray Nicholls bats, then became a social worker in the Midlands, coached in South Africa and worked in a public school in Wolverhampton.

Nicholas Jason Speak
RHB & LB, 1997-2001

100 GREATS

The pressures of captaincy effectively ended Nick Speak's Durham career after he was brought in for the retired David Boon in 2000.

In the new division one, Durham was out of its depth, particularly without talisman Boon and with the pace bowlers all injured at one time or another.

Speak began brightly with the gold award for his 72 in the BHC win over Yorkshire.

Then he suffered the ignominy of averaging 8.18 in his first 11 Championship innings and 'began to lose the faith of some players', wrote Tim Wellock in Wisden. He also lost the toss eight times in the first nine games and took the blame for enforcing the follow on against Yorkshire at Headingley in early July, when the Tykes scored 386/4 in the second innings.

The turning point came in August when Durham lost by 232 runs at Derby after leading by only 144 runs with four wickets standing on the second day. Opposing captain Dominic Cork (200*) hit 95 in

Nicholas Jason Speak
Born: Manchester, 21 November 1966
Also played for: Lancashire

Batting

M	I	NO	Runs
54	93	13	2,292
Ave	100	50	
28.65	3	13	

Bowling

O	Md	R	W	Ct
6	0	27	0	24

Best Performance
124* v. Cambridge University, 1997

63 deliveries on the third morning and set Durham 500 to win. The defeat 'provoked a huge row, after which the captain's position was felt to be untenable,' said Wellock.

With coach Norman Gifford seeing out his final month, new chairman Bill Midgley concentrating in the inaugural Riverside one-day internationals and Geoff Cook re-instated as director of cricket, Durham's management was in flux. Speak did not find favour with new coach Martyn Moxon and played just two Championship games in 2001.

Speak had arrived at Durham with Martin Speight for the 1997 season, heralded as a major signing to shore up a failing batting side. He'd hit 1,892 runs in 1992, including 232 against Leicestershire, but, like Speight, Mike Roseberry and many of the 1992 newcomers, his play was already declining before he arrived.

In June 1997 he hit a century against Cambridge University, but averaged just 16 in the Championship. In 1998 he scored 638 runs at 27.73 and in 1999, when not suffering from nerve damage to his left leg, was able to hit two centuries, including a Championship best of 110* against Gloucestershire. But the captaincy wrecked his form, although the likeable Lancastrian battled back to second top of the 2000 averages. It was all in vain as Jon Lewis took the captaincy and Speak had to think of life after cricket.

Martin Peter Speight

RHB & WK, 1997-2001

100 GREATS

Durham has at least two cricketing artists. More talented with the brushes than well-known dauber Jack Russell, if less able behind the stumps, Martin Speight was an eccentric wicket-keeper batsman for Durham who failed to fulfil his potential, but was always ready with a scheme.

Speight used to change his hairstyle yearly, a neat side parting giving way to dreadlocks, then to blond highlights. Perhaps this and his estuary English accent reflected a rebellion against his elevated schooling at Hurstpierpoint College and Durham University. Speight came to prominence for Sussex with a delightfully aggressive half century to set the tone in the 1993 NWT final, which produced a record 643 runs. He hit 1,375 runs in 1990 and was

one of the most attractive shotmakers not to play from England in the early 1990s. However, a severe viral infection halted his progress in 1995 and he moved to Durham for 1997.

Speight rarely kept for Sussex, but was employed in the wicketkeeper/batsman role at Durham, where he was attracted by his happy memories of student days. The 5ft 9in shotmaker never re-captured his old batting form, but did set Durham records for catches in a season (61 in 1998) and a career (197 including three as a fielder).

He never made a century for Durham having hit 13 (and three one-day) hundreds for Sussex. Twice Speight came close, once unselfishly and intelligently shielding Steven Lugsden in a match-saving

Martin Peter Speight
Born: Walsall, 24 October 1967
Also played for: Sussex

Batting

M	I	NO	Runs	
70	117	16	2,411	
Ave	100	50	Ct	St
23.87	0	13	192	5

Best Performances
97* v. Hampshire, 1998
97 v. Glamorgan, 1999

tenth wicket partnership of 61 against Hampshire.

Andrew Pratt, a better stumper, replaced Speight in 2001, though Speight won occasional selection as a batsman. Durham released the cheerful ancient history graduate at the end of the season and he became a Northumberland player and sport development officer in South Northumberland.

Richard Thompson Spooner
LHB & WK, 1946-47

Richard Thompson Spooner
Born: Stockton-on-Tees, 30 December 1919
Died: Torquay, 20 December 1997
Also played for: Warwickshire, England

Batting

M	I	NO	Runs	
17	23	2	473	
Ave	100	50	Ct	St
22.52	0	3	12	21

Best Performance
89 v. Northumberland, 1946

The third of Durham's former players (after Cecil Parkin and David Townsend) to play for England, Dick Spooner was 32, with just four years of first-class experience when he won national recognition.

Debuting for Durham in 1946 the flat-nosed, hard-hitting Spooner scored 291 runs at 26.45 as Durham finished 12th in the Championship. In 1947 he scored another 182 runs. But it was his wicketkeeping that attracted Warwickshire's attention, particularly his 21 stumpings in 17 games, which included India's Rudi Modi and Vinoo Mankad at Ashbrooke in 1946.

The Norton club player went to Edgbaston with Durham team-mate Alan Townsend in 1948, possibly through a link arranged by Norton-born triple blue Mickey Walford. Durham wicketkeeper Jack Fox followed Spooner in 1959, the year Spooner retired. Warwickshire's Clive Leach came to Durham in return in 1955.

An aggressive left-handed opener, Spooner topped Warwickshire's averages in the title winning season of 1951 with 1,767 Championship runs, including four centuries.

He went on the Commonwealth tour to India playing in all five tests, scoring 71 and 92 in the draw at Calcutta. England won the next test, at Kanpur, but Spooner's 66 could not stop a loss at Madras. With Godfrey Evans the incumbent Spooner played only two more tests, both when Evans was injured, one against the West Indies in 1953/54 and one against South Africa in 1955, when he scored a pair but conceded no byes. However, in his England career he let 46 byes in seven games and selectors preferred Evans for his tidier keeping.

Not to be confused with Lancashire (1899-1921) and England (1905-12) stylist Reggie (R.H.) Spooner, Dick (R.T.) Spooner was Durham's most successful Test player during the forty years between Cecil Parkin and Colin Milburn's international careers. Loud on the field and a good team man, Spooner retired to become a groundsman in Devon.

He remembered as a small boy at Norton CC, as darkness approached, 'you were given the chance to bat wearing men's pads which rubbed under your chin'. Spooner also thanked the NYSD league for his schooling in cricket and David Townsend and Johnny Prest for stepping down to Norton II to give him a first team chance.

Michael Tate
RHB & OB, 1952-68

100 GREATS

Leading the way, through a link with Frank Tyson, Durham was fortunate not to lose Mike Tate to Northamptonshire in the 1950s as it subsequently lost Gus Williamson, Malcolm Scott and Colin Milburn. Tate made his name by taking seven wickets in a school's match at Lord's as a teenager. His off spin supported Yorkshire opening bowlers Alec Coxon and Ron Aspinall in the early 1950s before he left to play for Northants in 1954 and 1955. However, he only made the second team, kept out by Australian left armer off break and chinaman bowler George Tribe, who took 176 wickets in 1955. 'You soon find out if you're going to make it', he said. 'You need tunnel vision and your face has got to fit. Northants were more interested in left armers. Durham had lots of potential county cricketers who didn't want to go first-class. And Jack Iley was happy that Durham was not first-class. He thought we were doing well enough.'

Tate roomed at Northants with former Durham University student Frank Tyson, who recommended Tate to the first-class county. Tate said: 'After Frank returned from Australia I asked him to bowl me a few off spinners in the nets. They were the fastest off spinners I've ever seen. I wouldn't like to say today there was anyone near his speed.'

Ampleforth educated, Tate was a productive bowler for Middlesbrough in the NYSD League, taking eight wickets in an innings in 1958 and 1959, when the club won the second of four Championships in five seasons. He later nurtured the Old brothers into the Middlesbrough team.

Short and stocky, Tate was Durham captain for part of 1960 when Don Hardy was unavailable. In

Michael Tate
Born: Middlesbrough, 2 August 1932

Batting			
M	I	NO	Runs
54	60	12	667
Ave	100	50	
13.89	0	2	

Bowling			
O	Md	R	W
964.2	202	2,725	121
Ave	5wI	10wM	Ct
21.28	5	0	19

Best Performances
73 v. Lancashire II, 1961
5/37 v. Cumberland, 1961

1961 he was at his peak taking over 20 wickets at under 20, as part of a promising side that included young players Russell Inglis, Alan Burridge and Stuart Young. Throughout the 1960s Tate played intermittently, as the county struggled to make an impact in the Minor Counties Championship. Tate had bowled economically against India at Ashbrooke in 1952 and was the sole survivor from that team when he took 3/45, the best in the match, against Pakistan in 1962. However, he was not used for the GC games that effectively superseded the tourist matches from 1964.

Tate, a farmer at Bishopton, later took up painting and a watercolour by him is on a wall in the Riverside pavilion.

James Thackeray
LHB & LFM, 1905-14

James Thackeray
Born: Hebbum Quay, 1881
Died: Hebbum, November 1968

Batting

M	I	NO	Runs
70	111	32	763
Ave	100	50	
9.65	0	1	

Bowling

O	Md	R	W
1,153	225	3,167	176
Ave	5wl	10wM	Ct
17.99	10	3	50

Best Performances
50 v. Cheshire, 1909
8/40 v. Northumberland, 1910

Footballer Jimmy Thackeray enjoyed his summers almost as much as his winters, forming an important part of the Durham attack in the decade before the First World War.

Thackeray, son of a docker, played with Alf Common, brother of Johnny Common, Durham wicketkeeper from 1910-25. Alf, the first £1,000 football transfer, had winger Thackeray to thank for laying on many of his goals, while left arm swing bowler Thackeray applauded Johnny for catches made off his bowling behind the stumps.

Dark-haired and swarthy with staring eyes, he took 11/129 v. Northumberland 1905 and bowling with Alf Morris and George Turnbull took five wickets in each innings (10/76 in the match) in the 1908 win at Wearmouth v. Lancashire II.

In tourist matches, Thackeray the trier showed his determination with nought and 38 and 1/69 against South Africa in 1907 when Durham lost by an innings and 29 and 3/50 opening bowling at Ashbrooke v. All India in 1911. In 1910 he took 32 of his 37 wickets that season in his last four matches, including 8/40 and 2/52 in the win over Northumberland at Chester-le-Street, where he was the professional. He played for South Shields from 1905-07, Chester-le-Street in 1908, Middlesbrough in 1909 and returned to Chester-le-Street from 1910-14.

Thackeray was one of the players Durham missed after the First World War, along with Tommie Bradford (in the Army), Hughie Dales (Middlesex), Adamson (died in action), Alf Morris (retired) and Frank Harry (Worcestershire). Thackeray worked as a groundsman at Reyrolles in Hebburn.

Alan Townsend
RHB & RM, 1942-47

Alan Townsend
Born: Stockton-on-Tees, 28 August 1921

Batting

M	I	NO	Runs
19	21	2	393
Ave	100	50	
20.68	0	1	

Bowling

O	Md	R	W
54.4	4	3,167	10
Ave	Ct		
21.60	5		

Best Performance
86 v. Northumberland, 1947

So fully did Alan Townsend integrate himself into the Warwickshire cricket scene, he won election to the Warwickshire CCC committee and a place in Robert Brooke's top 100 Warwickshire cricketers. For Durham, Townsend showed early promise as an all-rounder in three games in 1943. An early influence was father figure Jack Carr, who was by then almost 50 years old.

Townsend played for Thornaby from 1942-45, and was Eppleton professional in 1947.

His stylish and unhurried batting returned 233 runs at 25.88 in 1947, with fellow Stockton player Dick Spooner hitting 291 at 26.45. However, like Spooner, it wasn't batting that made Townsend stand out. He was an exceptional slip fielder and went on to take 409 catches in 340 games for Warwickshire. He also bowled medium paced inducers. Townsend's best batting effort for Durham was 86 out of 202 on poor batting pitch at Ashbrooke in a win over Northumberland.

Aged 26, he moved to Edgbaston with Spooner. Both were from Stockton, had played 19 and 17 games respectively Durham, and played 340 and 312 for Warwickshire, who they helped win the 1951 Championship.

Townsend was often involved in run out muddles

and is pictured in 1950s Warwickshire captain Tom Dollery's autobiography running to the same end as Dollery. He once told Swaranjit Singh to look for three, only for fielder Cyril Poole to pick up and throw just as Singh finished his second. He dutifully set off for a third with the ball already in wicket-keeper Geoff Millman's gloves and was duly run out.

While Spooner found success with England,

Townsend, despite scoring 1,000 runs in season five times with a best of 1,227 at 29.92 in 1953 often disappointed with the bat and had a career average of 24.95 for 11,965 runs. But his catching, wickets (323 at 28.70), patient coaching of young-sters and committee service made up a wide contri-bution at Warwickshire, albeit one Durham could have done with in the 1950s and 1960s.

David Charles Humphery Townsend
RHB & RM, 1935-50

100 GREATS

David Charles Humphery Townsend
Born: Norton-on-Tees, 20 April 1912
Died: Norton-on-Tees, 27 January 1997
Also played for: Oxford University, England

Batting

M	I	NO	Runs
40	55	3	1,451
Ave	100	50	
27.90	4	5	

Bowling

O	Md	R	W
72.4	17	190	9
Ave	Ct		
21.11	18		

Best Performance
138* v. New Zealand, 1937

The first current Durham player to play test cricket, David Townsend was the last man to be picked for England without playing for a first-class county.

However, it was his Oxford University form that won him a place on the 1934/35 MCC tour to the West Indies, where he opened in three Tests.

Uniquely, four generations of the Townsend family played first-class cricket. Grandfather Frank played for Gloucestershire (1870-91), and father Charles Lucas also represented Grace's county (1893-1922), as well as playing twice for England. Charles' brothers (David's uncles) Frank Norton Townsend (1896-1900) and Arthur (1903-10) played for Gloucestershire. David's son Jon played for Oxford University (and Durham) in 1964.

David Townsend played cricket at Winchester School, then missed out in his first summer at Oxford due to illness. In 1933 he scored 734 runs including 195 against the Free Foresters and 72* on his first-class debut against Yorkshire. The next season he hit 193 in front of some influential judges

in the University match at Lord's.

Wisden said Townsend had patience, power, range of stroke (he drove, pulled and hooked force-fully) and fine physique. On the West Indies tour his innings high of 36 out of 107 on his Test debut was his only notable score. England's weak team lost two and drew one of the three Tests he played.

He returned to Norton, where he practised as a solicitor in the family law firm at Stockton for half a century. Aloof, wealthy and sometimes arrogant, Townsend was born and died in a house overlook-ing Norton CC in Station Road.

Debuting for Durham against South Africa in 1935 and top scoring with 48 in the second innings of the innings and 45 run loss, Townsend played his first Championship game three weeks later alongside Cambridge blue Mickey Walford. Walford, also from Norton, became a teacher at Sherborne and England rugby trialist, hockey international and Somerset cricketer.

After touring with Martineau's side to Egypt in 1936, Townsend captained Durham regularly from 1937-47, succeeding, with 'Taffer' Charlton, ill Tom Dobson, who died four years later.

Tall, slim and steady, Townsend scored 138* against a weakened New Zealand attack in 1937. His other three centuries for Durham all came in 1938, when he was available all year and he scored 497 Championship runs and 533 in all at 35.50.

His club side, Norton won the NYSD League in 1935, 37, 38, 46, 49 and 51 with Townsend scoring eight centuries between these years, fourth for the club behind his father Charlie's 16.

After war service he led Durham to just one win in 1946, guiding the side home with 31* against Northumberland at Ashbrooke in a rain-reduced one-day match. Townsend scored 283 runs, second most behind his successor as captain Bill Proud, but broke a wrist early in the 1947 season, after which Durham lost Harold Stephenson, Dick Spooner, Alan Townsend to Somerset and Warwickshire. Townsend was increasingly unavailable and the county finished 16th, 16th and 22nd in his last three seasons. He returned to The Parks for his final first-class match for Free Foresters in 1948. He also played football as a centre half for Stockton.

100 GREATS

George Turnbull
RHB & RLB, 1897-1910

George Turnbull
Born: Washington, 1875
Died: At sea, off Salonika, Greece, 6 September 1917

Batting

M	I	NO	Runs
93	143	20	2,774
Ave	**100**	**50**	
22.55	3	14	

Bowling

O	Md	R	W
2,773.5	818	6,169	467
Ave	**5wI**	**10wM**	**Ct**
13.20	37	14	75

Best Performances
172 *v.* Northumberland, 1906
8/45 *v.* Northamptonshire, 1904

'One of the best all-round cricketers Durham ever had, and a native at that,' wrote Hon. Secretary William Bell.

George Turnbull set Durham's second best first-class bowling record, and was in the top five batting aggregates when he left England for South Africa before the First World War. The Craghead professional started unpromisingly, with seven and 0/58 in his single match in 1897, but progressed quickly. Often opening the bowling with his leg breaks; he took 52 wickets in 1898 and a Durham record 71 in 1899.

Having moved to Chester-le-Street for 1898 and Darlington for 1899-1901, he missed most of 1900,

when Durham shared the Championship. But in 1901, when Durham won outright, he scored his first century, 103 against Northants at Northampton and took 56 wickets at 10.46 in the season and averaged 27.12 with his aggressive slogging, with a top score of 73.

Distinctive with his handlebar moustache and sturdy frame, in 1901 he took 46 wickets, 40 in the championship, as Durham shared the title. He took over 50 wickets in 1903 and in 1905, 55. That season Durham boasted five of its dozen most prolific wicket takers in William Whitwell, John Gregory, John Butler and Alf Morris.

In 1903 he topped the Minor Counties bowling averages with 53 wickets for 424 runs, taking 11 wickets in the match against Yorkshire II, Northumberland and Cambridge. He took 11 three more times in his career and 12/118, his best, in 1904, against Northumberland. In 1904 Turnbull had stepped up to be the side's best all-rounder, with 56 wickets at 10.46 and a batting average of 27.12, all in eight games. In 1907, Elliot's last season, Turnbull was playing second fiddle to Morris, taking 37 wickets at 15.1, compared to Morris' 64 at 12.40.

Durham's administration, recognising the influence of Turnbull and Morris, paid £100 more than the season before to the professionals.

Turnbull was also an excellent, aggressive right hand batsman, who rose up the order as his career went on. His Durham centuries were 103 *v.* Northamptonshire in 1901, 172 *v.* Northumberland 1906 (Durham's joint second best with William Copeland *v.* Northumberland 1885 and behind Edgar Elliot) and 113 *v.* Staffordshire in 1910, after Sydney Barnes had taken 8/16 in Durham's first innings.

He specialised in the rearguard actions, in 1908 making 97 with Durham six wickets down against Yorkshire II in its second innings, leading by 20 runs. Turnbull and his captain Ernest Proud added 178 for the seventh wicket, the tail put on 67 more and Durham won by 154 runs. He took 3/65 and 4/15 in the game too.

In 1909 Morris took 10/91 in the win over Cheshire, with Turnbull taking nine of the other 10 wickets to fall, but Durham won just two games out of ten with the glory years of 1900 and 1901 were over.

Turnbull was professional with Craghead in 1897, Chester-le-Street (1898), Darlington (1899-1901), Nelson (Lancashire League) from 1902-06, Burnmoor (1907-08) and Enfield (Lancashire League) from 1909-10. Turnbull's move to Enfield prevented further Durham appearances.

Later he emigrated to coach at King Williamstown in South Africa, where he had coached in the winters.

He died at sea close to where C.Y. Adamson perished while serving in the First World War.

Jack Watson

LHB & RM/OB, 1945-66

This robust all-rounder was as versatile as Gary Sobers, and made some Sobers-like impressions for Durham in a long career interrupted by 67 matches with Northumberland.

A journeyman professional for Ryton, Durham City, Ashington, Alnwick, Shildon BR, Blackhall, Swalwell and Normanby Hall, Watson made his Durham debut in 1945, ending the season with 13 wickets at 9.46 with his fast medium bowling.

In 1956 he returned from Northumberland for nine more seasons with Durham, winning his cap straight away. He took 92 wickets in the last two, including 52 at 12.76 in 1964 aged 43. He took seven in the win over Staffordshire, 10 against Yorkshire II, eight in a win over Northumberland, nine in the win over Cumberland and eight in the draw with Yorks.

Against India in 1959, Watson took 6/23 and 3/46 off 34.2 overs with 13 maidens in his first tourist match, as well as scoring 15 and 11*. Bowling spin he took Durham close to victory, with India needing 239 from 51 overs, he had Chandra Borde (81) and Kripal Singh (32) caught by Leach, but India ended 28 short with three wickets standing.

He made the first Gillette Cup win in 1964, then took 0/63 off 13 and scored two not out in the second round loss to Sussex.

Watson played on into his seventies for Hunwick,

Jack Watson			
Born: High Spen, 17 April 1921			

Batting

M	I	NO	Runs
128	161	41	2,792
Ave	100	50	
23.26	0	10	

Bowling

O	Md	R	W	Ave
2,779.1	891	6,499	392	16.57
5wI	10wM	Ct	St	
25	5	84	1	

Best Performances
73 v. Staffordshire, 1958
8/88 v. Staffordshire, 1963

heading the bowling averages, still heading the bowling averages in his sixties.

He played for Minor Counties against the tourists and for Northumberland in 67 matches, scoring 1,630 runs and taking 195 wickets.

His best years were 1964 with 52 wickets, 1959 with 36, 1956 with 38, 1960 with 40, 1963 with 29, and 1965 with 40 wickets and 313 runs when he stepped in as captain when Hardy was unavailable.

Lyndon Herbert Weight
RHB & RM, 1913-27

Lyndon Herbert Weight
Born: Newport, 20 January 1889
Died: Durham City, 13 January 1973

Batting

M	I	NO	Runs
68	118	6	2,725
Ave	100	50	
24.33	6	7	

Bowling

O	Md	R	W
1,109.2	299	2,961	165
Ave	5wI	10wM	Ct
17.94	9	3	29

Best Performances
123 *v.* Cheshire, 1920
7/65 *v.* Northumberland, 1923

L en Weight 'gave whole-hearted service to the county,' said Hon. Secretary William Bell. Weight's record shows he was one of the finest pre-1939 all-rounders. Weight was sixth in the Durham batting and bowling career aggregates when Bell wrote his remark shortly after he retired. Welshman Weight played for the county in 1913 even before he was qualified, but in a friendly against Northampton. He qualified in 1920, but made way for younger batsmen after 1927. In between he consistently contributed to the county cause even as the team struggled, reaching a low of 20th in 1924. That year Weight was ever present as Durham won two out of eight, scoring 346 runs and taking 37 wickets at 14.72. Jack Carr, who eventually took Weight's all-round place, made his first appearance and Durham quickly improved to 13th in 1925 and the title in 1926.

Weight was professional at Hendon in 1913, South Shields from 1920-22, Sunderland 1923-26, and Boldon afterwards. Those were the days of great crowds hoping for a Durham upset in tourist matches, and Weight responded to the challenge. Opening the bowling against West Indies in 1923 at Feethams, Weight took 3/51 and 4/41 (all bowled), but, batting at No.4 Learie Constantine bowled him for a duck in the first innings and eight wickets fell for 39 while he scored 13* in the second innings. Durham lost by 280 runs. Weight opened against the 1924 South Africans, top scoring with 43 in the rain-affected draw at

Sunderland. In his last tourist match in 1926, Australian Charlie Macartney dismissed Weight for four and 22, and his bowling was hardly used by Bertie Brooks.

After a quarter of a century of waiting, Durham won the Minor County Championship that year, with Weight retiring a season later. After coming fifth in his debut year, tenth place in 1922 was the best Durham managed during Weight's 10 seasons at Durham until 1926, when the post-war coaching scheme paid off as Maurice Nichol and Harry Gibbon stepped up to help old pros like Weight. That year, major contributions from Weight included 100 *v.* Northumberland and a stand of 170 with Cecil Ferens for the first wicket against Yorkshire II.

The highest stand he'd been part of was of 223 for the second wicket with Brooks in 1922, against Northumberland, when he had also hit a century in the return game. He added another against the neighbours in 1925 and a fourth in 1926. His two seven-wicket innings analyses were against Northumberland too, adding 5/19 in the other innings in 1920, when he returned a career best 12/87. He took 11/107 in 1921 and 10/34 in 1924, both against Lancashire II. His best bowling figures came against the same side, 12/87 in 1920.

Weight was later a respected coach with young county players.

William Fry Whitwell

RHB & RFM, 1887-1902

William Fry Whitwell
Born: Stockton-on-Tees, 12 December 1867
Died: Newcastle-upon-Tyne, 12 April 1942
Also played for: Yorkshire

Batting

M	I	NO	Runs
69	103	10	1,190
Ave	100	50	
12.79	0	2	

Bowling

O	Md	R	W
2,384.1	745	5,401	355
Ave	5wI	10wM	Ct
15.21	32	15	31

Best Performances
69 v. Staffordshire, 1895
8/18 v. Lincolnshire, 1895

The Whitwell brothers were educated at Uppingham School in Rutland, excelling at games. They were an early product of the school's fine cricket tradition. England cricketers Percy Chapman, Jonathan Agnew and James Whitaker were all Uppingham pupils. The Whitwell family owned Thornaby Ironworks and lived in a fine house, Overdene at Saltburn.

William Whitwell was a better cricketer than younger brother Joseph. A fast bowler rather than a batsman, he led Durham from 1893-96 – Durham's fourth captain.

Untiring and capable, his off cutters and seamers brought him his wickets and an opportunity with Yorkshire, given by Lord Hawke despite Whitwell being born outside the county boundary. He was one of just 23 unqualified cricketers who played for Yorkshire until it changed its rules before the 1993 season. Durham-born Cec Parkin was another, in 1906.

Hon. Secretary Harry Mallett spoke forcibly about Whitwell's non-native status at Durham's AGM in April 1890, but Yorkshire ignored its own rule. Whitwell returned to play for Durham in 1891 anyway. Joseph was qualified through being born at Saltburn-by-the-Sea, though is listed in some publications as Saltburn-born. William played 10 games as an amateur under a residential qualification, toured North America with another of the twenty-three aliens, Gainsborough-born Yorkshire captain Lord Hawke, in 1894 and finished his first-class career with the Gentlemen in 1900.

In club cricket he took 9-40 for Norton v. Darlington 1899, 8-33 v. Redcar in 1898 when

Norton won the NYSD. He switched to Saltburn from its 1905 debut season, when the club finished bottom, with one win.

For Durham he often carried the bowling, taking 12-55 off 50.2 overs at Norton against Warwickshire in an 18 run win in 1891, when he bowled unchanged through both innings. He took seven in an innings 11 times, one less than Morris' record, including five in friendlies and three against Northumberland. From 1889-99, he took 12 in a match five times; with 12-53 against Yorkshire II in 1899 his best, and 11 three times with 11-58 against Northants the best. He also took 10 wickets seven times, including 10-37 against Lincolnshire in 1895.

He took 58 wickets at 13.84 under his brother's leadership in 1899, and 35 at 11.22 in 1900 as Durham won the Championship jointly with Glamorgan and Northants.

He held the Durham wicket taking record on retirement in 1902, which was passed by only Morris and Turnbull before the First World War.

Whatever made William's brother Joseph kill himself aged 63 is not recorded. What is, is Joseph's successful record as a Durham captain that made cricket a popular game in the industrialised county. The tall opener had led Durham from 1899-1902, winning the Minor County Championship in 1900 and 1901. He shot himself in the family home, Langbaurgh Hall, Great Ayton, in Yorkshire's North Riding in 1932.

William Whitwell died in Newcastle during the Second World War aged 75, nine years after his brother.

John Stuart Wilkinson
RHB & RFM, 1968-85

John Stuart Wilkinson
Born: Ebchester, 18 October 1942
Also played for: Minor Counties

Batting

M	I	NO	Runs
90	49	12	252
Ave			
6.81			

Bowling

O	Md	R	W
1,880.3	531	4,721	237
Ave	5wI	10wM	Ct
19.91	9	0	22

Best Performance
7/49 v. Northumberland, 1978

Ebchester, the Anglo-Saxon named Romano-British town on Dere Street, produced the rugged Viking-like figure of blond, droopily moustached Stuart Wilkinson (*top right*), one of Durham's finest home-born fast bowlers. The tearaway opening right-armer made his county debut when playing for Shotley Bridge (1968-69). He later played for Durham City (1971-74) and Philadelphia (1975-78), returning to Shotley Bridge in 1979.

He effectively replaced Stuart Young as Durham's spearhead in the late 1960s.

Wilkinson played for Minor Counties from 1977-79 and for Minor Counties (East) and (North) in the Benson and Hedges Cup. Wilkinson, with Peter Kippax and Neil Riddell from Durham, helped Minor Counties beat the Australians at Sunderland in 1977. Former Durham player David Bailey was the home captain. The Minor Counties beat New Zealand the following year in similar circumstances, chasing a 200 plus total after a generous declaration. Wilkinson also toured Kenya in 1978 in the Minor Counties team with Peter Kippax and Neil Riddell.

He played in all Durham's pre-first-class Gillette Cup wins, debuting in 1973, and bowling Yorkshire's Boycott for 14 for an impressive first wicket. He said it was a career high: 'We were the first Minor County to beat a first-class one. Everyone went quickly home because we all had club cricket the following day. There was no big celebration, though we had a civic reception later. It started a good period for Durham. We became the best Minor County and it was the start of the push to go first-class.'

Always a strong performer on the bigger stage,

particularly when he matured as a bowler during the 1970s, Wilkinson won the Man of the Match award with 5/24 in the three-wicket loss to Northants in 1977. It was Durham's best in the competition until Australian Simon Davis' 7-32 in 1983. Neil Riddell, another late developer as a cricketer, said Wilkinson frightened the life out of Northants. He also praised Wilkinson's endurance and penetration on a baking hot day at Durham the following season, when Wilkinson bowled his best ever for 7/49. 'The fastest around', said team mate David O'Sullivan.

He dismissed England's best batsman Boycott again in 1978, taking 1/46, then returned 2/32 in the win over Berkshire in 1979, and 1/43 (Jim Love) in a four-wicket loss to Yorkshire 1979.

Recalled in 1984 aged 42, Wilkinson won the Man of the Match award against Cheshire in the Championship decider, taking 2/5 off seven overs. He retired after 1985, having played in all Durham's major triumphs of its most successful era.

Wilkinson played club cricket at Shotley Bridge until he was fifty-five, lasting long enough to appear with a teenage Paul Collingwood.

'I developed fairly late as a bowler, though I was always fairly quick. I had a unique action, energetic I think, not the classic fast bowler's action, with my feet doing all sorts of things – idiosyncratic, but it was mine, it was never coached.'

His captain Neil Riddell said: 'The best amateur bowler I played with or against. On his day he was brilliant and had the rare ability to move the ball around for long periods without sacrificing pace. He was always sharp enough, but what control he had, simply the best.'

Lance Cairns said 'Wilky' could have made a

first-class career, despite his quirks. Wilkinson said: 'We didn't know how, but if somebody had asked when I was eighteen I probably would. As a civil servant the financial reward was not there later.'

Cairns said: 'The unwritten word in the Durham camp was you could never ever talk about Wilky's hairpiece, so nobody ever did. He had a round

arm action that said he shouldn't be able to bowl quickly, but he could and he could have easily played county cricket. Most good sides have got to have a strike bowler and Wilky was ours. A very serious guy, but off the paddock he enjoyed a pint.'

Wilkinson no longer watches much cricket, saying: 'It's a bit late for itchy feet.'

John Gordon Barkass Williamson ———————— 100

RHB & RFM, 1954-69

GREATS

Gus Williamson's eclectic career began at Norton CC, from where he made his Durham debut aged eighteen in 1954.

He played for three seasons before National Service, when he played for the Combined Services in a first-class match in 1958. He then joined Northants, playing from 1959-62, with a highest score of 106* v. Cambridge University and best bowling of 6/47 v. Kent in 1959.

After his release Williamson ('one of the crafty ones who got out quick' said Malcolm Scott) joined Bishop Auckland as professional scoring over 400 runs (best 625 in 1966 when Bishops won the NYSD League) and taking over 40 wickets (best 88 in 1967) each season up to 1968. He scored 3,158 runs and took 425 wickets in six seasons for Bishops before returning to Norton. He then moved to Macclesfield CC and Cheshire.

For Durham he had the chastening figures of 1/122 off 17 overs opening the bowling as South Africa made 543 in the 1955 innings win at Ashbrooke. That year, when he was still a teenager, Williamson led the county pace bowlers with 32 wickets at 21.09. Malcolm Scott headed the bowling averages, but the promising pair soon left for National Service and Northamptonshire, robbing Durham of their best cricketing years.

Tall and wavy-haired, Williamson scored a first-class century, but rarely made runs in big games, scoring nought and one in his only tourist game. On his return to the county in 1963 he proved useful in the Gillette Cup, taking 2/13 in the 1964 win over Hertfordshire and shifting West Indies wicketkeeper Deryck Murray in the near miss in

John Gordon Barkass Williamson
Born: Norton, 4 April 1936
Also played for: Northants, Cheshire

Batting

M	I	NO	Runs
63	84	12	1,075
Ave	100	50	
14.93	0	3	

Bowling

O	Md	R	W
1,256.3	348	3,387	149
Ave	5wI	10wM	Ct
22.73	6	0	16

Best Performances
81 v. Staffordshire, 1955
7/62 v. Lancashire II, 1963

1967 against Nottinghamshire.

His best effort came in his last big game for Durham, when aged 32 and bowling fourth change, he removed Tom Graveney, Roy Booth, future Durham coach Norman Gifford and Vanburn Holder for 13 runs in 10.2 overs against Worcestershire in 1968 on a dodgy Ropery Lane pitch.

Durham, however, was skittled for 82, falling 17 runs short of an inaugural victory over a first-class county. He changed his name from Williamson, adding his family surname as stipulated by the terms of an inheritance, in 1965.

John Wood
Born: Wakefield, 22 July 1970
Also played for: Lancashire

Batting

M	I	NO	Runs
88	132	20	1,335
Ave	100	50	
11.91	0	2	

Bowling

O	Md	R	W
2,313.2	402	8,519	260
Ave	5wI	10wM	Ct
32.76	11	0	23

Best Performances
63* v. Nottinghamshire, 1993
7/58 v. Yorkshire, 1999

In just 21 deliveries fast bowler John Wood made a first truly decisive contribution for Durham after eight years on the staff.

With Simon Brown injured, Wood took four wickets in 21 balls as Warwickshire lost six wickets for 22 runs on a deteriorating Chester-le-Street pitch. This finished off Durham's promotion rivals and took the county into the first division in its first year of existence.

Injury-prone Wood had been a Durham hope since leading the 1992 averages with 16 wickets at 31.87, with a best of 5/68 against Hampshire. Even then captain David Graveney said Wood's 'rare natural ability' would need 'a strict off-season programme to improve his fitness'.

Recommended to Durham by Peter Kippax from the Bradford League, Wood played for Griqualand West in the Nissan Shield in 1990/91, but couldn't win a Yorkshire contract. Instead he trialed for Durham in 1991, taking 30 wickets at 30.76 in 17 matches and winning a contract for the inaugural first-class season.

Educated at Leeds Polytechnic, where he passed a BTEC Diploma and HND in Electrical and Electronic Engineering, Wood played for Tawa in New Zealand from 1993-95 to gain experience and keep fit off-season.

After promising to break through by taking 14 wickets at 21.64 at the start of 1995 he sustained a stress fracture of lower spine and missed all but the first four games. He'd shown his increasing endurance with 6-110 v. Essex at Stockton 1994,

and said the year out of game 'made me realise how much I love it'. He'd played just 36 first-class games in five seasons.

After 11 wickets at 43.27 in 1997, Wood needed to improve form and fitness in 1998, when eight players were to leave the club in a staff clean out. Wood responded, taking 61 wickets at 29.50, leading the attack in the absence of Brown. He took 36 at 22.58 in 1999 including his career best 7/58 in an innings loss to his native Yorkshire at Leeds and match figures of 8/97 in a victory against Warwickshire that helped secure the promotion, finally clinched by a quick single from the hefty Wood against Leicestershire- 'the abiding memory of my time at Durham'.

After not always being selected in 1999, in 2000 he took 33 wickets at 27.81, with three bags of five in an innings. Nevertheless, he decided to leave at the end of the year, disillusioned by Boon's departure and a management reshuffle that brought back Cook and brought in Martyn Moxon as coach.

Initially denied a release from the final year of his contract, Durham management let Wood go after Lancashire's approach. The move was initially unsuccessful – he took nine wickets for 511 runs in seven Championship games in 2001, though was a one-day regular.

He said: 'I'll always be grateful to Durham for giving me a chance.'

Stuart Harrison Young —————————————————

LHB & RFM, 1956-72

Often described as the best fast bowler in Minor Counties cricket never to have played for a first-class county, why did Stuart Young never move up?

Lance Cairns said: 'The makeup of the area meant jobs were pretty hard to come by. Also, they'd say if they were going to county fringe player with a contract for a year or two, then what happens to them? Most in Durham team had their work and were more than happy with the security of a job.'

Tall and thickset, Young turned professional at eighteen, when he also made his Durham debut. Seemingly a certainty for Northamptonshire's interest, he decided to work in colliery offices, and play as professional in the summer. He represented Horden Colliery Welfare in 1957-58, Chester-le-Street 1959-60, hometown Blackhall 1961, Darlington from 1962-69, South Shields in 1970, Philadelphia 1971-2, Bishop Auckland in 1973 as professional and as an amateur until his retirement in 1977.

He showed his class with two Gillette Man of the Match awards and success in his Minor Counties appearances against touring teams from 1959-64 and in 1969. Mike Tate emphasised this, saying Young was 'equally as good as Harmison in every department'.

The promising trio of Young, Russell Inglis and Jackie Fox made their Durham debuts in 1956. Young took 3/25 against Lancashire II, and became the effective replacement of Ron Aspinall, then in his late thirties, who retired in 1957, when Young took over 20 wickets. Durham won just 12 games out of 72 in the years up to 1962, finishing 14th, 15th, 21st, 19th, 18th and 15th in Young's first five seasons.

However, under 1955-67 captain Don Hardy, Young developed his bowling and started to hit energetically down the order. The 1959 annual report said Young had taken a piece out of the new stand at Edgbaston with a big hit. In 1960 Young's best performance was 9/97 in the match at Workington against Cumberland, but Durham still lost to the weakest Minor County by two runs.

In 1961 Durham showed signs of revival, and Young again took over 20 cheap wickets. In 1962 he took his career best, that included a hat-trick, against a team including England past, Jack Ikin, and future, David Steele.

Young injured himself in the nets prior to the 1965 season. Durham failed to qualify for the 1965 and 1966 Gillette Cup and Young was injured

Stuart Harrison Young			
Born: Blackhall, 6 July 1938			
Also played for: Minor Counties			
Batting			
M	I	NO	Runs
115	134	34	1,864
Ave	100	50	
18.64	1	3	
Bowling			
O	Md	R	W
2,685.5	776	6,041	348
Ave	5wI	10wM	Ct
17.35	13	39	29
Best Performances			
129* v. Cumberland, 1965 (set 8th-wicket County record of 181 with David Branson) 8/21 v. Staffordshire, 1962			

again in 1967. In 1968 he returned with perhaps his best performance, shifting Worcestershire's Ron Headley, Duncan Fearnley, John Ormrod and Basil D'Oliveira for 17 runs in 12 overs. He had Worcestershire 18/4 and only Tom Graveney's 45 on a drying Chester-le-Street wicket took his side to 98 all out. It was 16 too many, despite Young at No.9 hitting 12, fifth most in the match.

In 1969 Young's injury problems did not help Durham's showing, as the county fell to 19th. At the time he formed a formidable attack for Darlington with Alan Johnson (Durham 1965-68) from 1964-69. Young took 385 wickets at 11.93 in his eight seasons at the NYSD league club. A powerful and fast scoring left hander, well mannered, with a fine attitude on the field, who set a good example to younger players, Young passed on his knowledge, and didn't complain at dropped catches.

He made one last appearance in his speciality, the Gillette Cup, in 1972's win over Oxfordshire, but missed the second round loss to Surrey and his county career virtually ended. In 1973 he took 118 wickets at 10.14, the second most in a season for Bishop Auckland, helping the club win the NYSD Championship and Aynsley-Johnson Cup. Even after finishing as a professional, Young contributed into his late thirties, but the pity remained he never tested himself at higher levels, where he could have been a success.